A LIVING MYSTERY:

The International Art & History of

CROCHET

By Annie Louise Potter

Library of Congress Cataloging-in-Publication data.

Potter, Annie Louise.
A LIVING MYSTERY: The International Art & History of Crochet.

CIP 90-85190

A LIVING MYSTERY: The International Art & History of Crochet.

ISBN 1-879409-00-3

TABLE OF CONTENTS

...A Sincere Welcome to the Wonderful World of Crochet. Whether you are just now developing your interest in its creative potential, or have been a life-long participant in the craft, you'll find "A LIVING MYSTERY: THE INTERNATIONAL ART & HISTORY OF CROCHET" a most interesting and thought-provoking exploration into the many mysteries of the subject.

This book will take you on a journey into the past. You will share the joys of fresh discoveries in our exploration. You will enjoy fresh insights into the dim recesses of time — indeed, from the very earliest beginnings of crochet as a unique handicraft art — and how techniques that led to its development were used by generations of people in far-flung corners of the globe thousands of years before the Birth of Christ.

While there are many books available on the general subject of crochet, virtually all of them provide instructions on technique, offer patterns for the crocheter, and deal mostly with design and fashion. Very few offer historical and creative perspectives on what just might be one of the oldest handicraft arts in the history of mankind.

The mysteries surrounding the subject of crochet are most intriguing. Tracing the history and the art back through time and across many continents has been a true labor of love. At times, frustrating. Often exhilarating. Always fascinating. In-depth research in many of the world's most complete libraries, a careful sifting through the many strands of evidence existing in museums and world-famous collections, and on occasion discovering something completely new for fresh interpretation and documentation, made this a most challenging and rewarding adventure. I know that you will find this journey into the heart of crochet history to be a fascinating experience. It is my hope that you will be able to share the excitement of new discovery and add new perspective to your understanding of crochet and how it blends with other very old handicraft traditions.

Most published sources on crochet give only passing mention to the history of crochet. Often, they suggest only that its history is "obscure," or that it has "probably been known since earliest times," or that "it is perhaps one of the most used, but least understood of the handicraft arts." Its history is often covered in little more than a footnote or two.

The lack of qualified historical evidence is one of the strands of mystery that is explored in "A LIVING MYSTERY: THE INTERNATIONAL ART & HISTORY OF CROCHET." Why has there been an absence of such material?

Crochet is easier to learn than most, if not all, of the lace arts. It has been practiced for centuries. Yet, there is a notable absence of early crochet pieces or samples in the museums of the world — even museums known for their collections of the textile arts.

There is also an absence of crochet tools or implements in the world's museums and collections. Tools made of wood, bone, ivory, bronze, silver, and other metals would most certainly survive, whereas many early pieces of actual crochet work would understandably be lost through decay or fragmentation as the fibers of materials used would simply not last through generations of time. Current literature on crochet also contains many different and often conflicting interpretations of crochet history. While we appreciate the efforts of others, historians of the subject are often divided as to workable theories about crochet. There is also a great deal of confusion in even the most basic fact information. "A LIVING MYSTERY: THE INTERNATIONAL ART & HISTORY OF CROCHET" is an attempt to sort out, document, and provide a fresh interpretation to a subject that is long overdue for new publication.

First, you will be taken on a journey through time — to the very earliest beginnings — and shown how creative artisans of the day were able to innovate and design useful and needed protective clothing, nets for fishing, and snares for catching small birds. You will discover how successive generations of people were able to fashion new designs by using different materials and lengths of fibers from plants, animals, and crops cultivated for the specific purposes of naalebinding, netting, weaving, hooking, looping, and creative ever-improved versions and techniques of the art.

Then, you will discover the art of crochet reaching its pinnacle of both design and technique through the work of Mlle. Eleonore Riego De La Branchardiere — a creative genius of the 1800s who brought crochet to new heights of world recognition as an art in its own right. Through her efforts, crochet reached such an epitome of perfection that her work has never been improved upon as a traditional art form.

Very much like Mlle. Riego, I also like to innovate — to make ideas come to life — to bring something fresh and new to the wonderful world of crochet. To do so while maintaining a solid bond and commitment to the ageless heritage and traditions of the crocheted art is a value that can not only be enjoyed and perfected, it can be shared — with you and millions of other crocheters throughout the world.

Unraveling other strands of mystery surrounding crochet involves an understanding of how sincere interest in the subject moves across cultural boundaries. Many countries of the world have expressed their ideas, attitudes, and beliefs through the works they perform with their hands and a crochet hook. True art reflects cultural heritage and distinctions without regard to race, creed, or social standing. You will discover the many similarities and differences in the crochet art that exist across continents and between nearby villages. True art is an expression of the soul. It is a means of communication between people, a source of individual and national pride.

While it is often tempting to force crochet history into some sort of box where it is easy to package, I have made every effort to avoid doing so in "A LIVING MYSTERY: THE INTERNATIONAL ART & HISTORY OF CROCHET." Here, you will be able to trace the chronology of crochet as a "living history." You will see it come to life through the people and cultural influences that were responsible for its main development.

Research is continuing. While "A LIVING MYSTERY: THE INTERNATIONAL ART & HISTORY OF CROCHET" opens many fresh opportunities for understanding, the mysteries persist.

Research for this new publication focused upon many sections of the world that until now have not been recognized at all for their significance to the true history of crochet. You will find fascinating stories from the very cradle of civilization that have never before been disclosed through international publication. While the contributions of such countries as France, Italy, Belgium, and other Western European Countries are well-known to the art of crochet, there are other places that better demonstrate its history. Following strands of research as they surfaced, "A LIVING MYSTERY: THE INTERNATIONAL ART & HISTORY OF CROCHET" explores the subject from tiny seashore communities and remote villages in such places as the South of Spain, Turkey, Greece, Yugoslavia, and Ireland.

Following trade routes and shipping lanes along the Aegean, Adriatic, Mediterranean, and North Seas, the history of crochet comes alive. Tiny villages discovered in such places are today dependent upon their skills of hand to produce fine laces and crochet for world markets. They bring a special pride and flavor to their astonishing skills that help document crochet as living history.

Meeting people who have worked crochet for all of their lives and who learned from grandparents — whose livelihood has been dependent upon their craft — has provided the means of separating vague legend from reality. Interviewing and learning from these proud people, some of whom have practiced their art for seventy or eighty years, also provided a fresh romantic feeling for crochet that simply cannot come from books alone.

Crochet as living history is now experiencing a revival of interest into the decade of the 1990s. In terms of the number of people being attracted to the craft each year, there has never been a time in history when the need for crochet as a means of individual expression has been more evident. Crochet is fun. It is flexible. It is only limited by the imagination of the creative designer or worker. It is easy to learn. Its possibilities are endless.

Welcome to the wonderful world of crochet. "A LIVING MYSTERY: THE INTERNATIONAL ART & HISTORY OF CROCHET" would not have been possible without active support, interest, and participation of all those museum curators, rare book librarians, national embassy staff members, and owners of private collections from throughout the world who are listed in my acknowledgments. I am grateful for their extremely valuable and qualified help.

Of special importance to this project have been the tireless efforts and continuing support of Mr. John Randolph Sauer, who not only encouraged me to publish this work — to turn a dream into a reality, but helped me guide its development through every major step.

Mr. Sauer assembled his top research, development and photographic task force headed by Dr. Deyrol E. Anderson (Ph.D.) and his associate, Ms. Shirley Ann Jurjovec. The task force spent countless hours checking and preparing information, searching through the libraries and museums of the world to establish the authenticity of this work. Their dedication calls for a special thank you.

A special mention must also be made of Mr. Arn Christian Sauer, a highly talented young photographer whose hard work and artistic eye has greatly enhanced the photographic content of this book.

And finally, a special acknowledgment to the vital role my beloved mother, Hilma Louise Gentry Potter, played. She taught me crochet as a young girl, encouraged my creativity in the arts, music and handicrafts and supported me in everything I did all of my life. I lost her last year. I miss her dearly.

MUSEUMS, CULTURAL INSTITUTIONS, AND NATIONAL ORGANIZATIONS:

Alfonso XIII, Sevilla, Spain
Alhambra Palace, Granada, Spain
American Craft Council, U.S.A.
Annie's Attic, Big Sandy, Texas, U.S.A.
Art Resource, New York, New York, U.S.A.
Benaki National Museum & Gallery, Athens, Greece
Bettmann Archive, New York, New York, U.S.A.
Biblioteca Ambrosiana, Milan, Italy
British National Museum, London, England
City of York Art Gallery, York, England
Colorado Historical Society, Denver, Colorado, U.S.A.
Cooper-Hewitt Museum, New York, New York, U.S.A.
Department of Irish Folklore, University College, Dublin, Ireland
Ditta Scala, Florence, Italy
Embassy of England
Embassy of Greece
Embassy of Ireland
Embassy of Spain
Embassy of Turkey
Embassy of United States, Milan, Italy
Embassy of Yugoslavia
Ethnographic Museum, Split, Yugoslavia
Ethnographic Museum, Zagreb, Yugoslavia
Gothic Cathedral, Sevilla, Spain
Greek Exports Promotion Organization, Athens, Greece
International Crochet Guild, Big Sandy, Texas, U.S.A.
Matica Iseljenika Hrvatska, Zagreb, Yugoslavia
Museum of Anthropology, Ethojrasski Musej, Belgrade, Yugoslavia
Museum Textil i del la Indumentaria, Barcelona, Spain
National Historical Museum, Athens, Greece
National Museum of Copenhagen, Copenhagen, Denmark
National Museum of Ireland, Dublin, Ireland
National Portrait Gallery, London, England
New York Metropolitan Museum, New York, New York, U.S.A.
Patronat Municipal De Turismo, Spain
Peabody Museum, Harvard University, Cambridge, Massachusetts, U.S.A.
Royal Dublin Society, Battsbridge, Dublin, Ireland
Royal Museum of England, Courtesy of The Queen, London, England
St. Mary's Church, Island of Pag, Pag, Yugoslavia
St. Steven's Cathedral, Zagreb, Yugoslavia
Santa Florentina Convent, Spain
Smithsonian Institute, Washington, D.C., U.S.A.
Strong Museum, Rochester, New York, U.S.A.

Turkish Radio & Television Corporation, Ankara, Turkey

Uffizi Gallery, Florence, Italy

United States Air Force Academy Research Library,
Colorado Springs, Colorado, U.S.A.

University of Southern Colorado, Department of Mass
Communications, Pueblo, Colorado, U.S.A.

University of Southern Colorado Research Library,
Pueblo, Colorado, U.S.A.

Victoria and Albert Museum, London, England

Volart Encajes Y Tejidos, S.A., (Lace Factory,
Barcelona, Spain)

Winterthur Museum - Gardens, Winterthur, Delaware, U.S.A.

SIGNIFICANT INDIVIDUALS PARTICIPATING IN RESEARCH AND LIAISON:

Ms. El Sanatlari Egitimi Bolumu, Gazi Univsersitesi,
Ankara, Turkey

Mr. Ante Buneta, Director, Matica Iseljenika Hrvatska,
Zagreb, Yugoslavia

Ms. Jeffrey Cobb, Research and Project Liaison to England,
Bellvue, Washington, U.S.A.

Ms. Breda Conway, Research Assistant and Liaison to Ireland,
Denver, Colorado, U.S.A.

Ms. Sylvia Cosh, Modern Crochet Designer, England

Ms. Nine Erdek, Research and Liaison to Turkey,
Ankara, Turkey

Ms. Eithne D'Arcy, Irish Lace Historian, Northern Ireland

Ms. Lale Rodriguez de Fashho, Liaison, Sevilla, Spain

Ms. Jean Drueszendow, New York Metropolitan Museum,
New York, New York, U.S.A.

Ms. Mesleki Egitim Fakultesi, Gazi Univsersitesi,
Ankara, Turkey

Ms. Lale Gingok, Mimar Sinan University of Istanbul,
Istanbul, Turkey

Ms. Eveline Greif, Arts Administration, Royal Dublin
Society, Dublin, Ireland

Professor Sukru Gurel, University of Denver, Visiting
Professor, University of Ankara, Turkey

Ms. Alice M. Jurjovec, Research Assistant and Liaison to
Yugoslavia, Canon City, Colorado, U.S.A.

Professor Dr. Firdeus Kaya, Gazi Universitesi,
Ankara, Turkey

Ms. Bernadette Kinery, Research Assistant and Liaison to
Ireland, Drishane, Killeagh, County Cork, Ireland

Ms. Sylvia Letcia, Research and Location Guide, Matica
Iseljenika Hrvatska, Zagreb, Yugoslavia

Mr. Nicholas Linardatos, Research Assistant & Embassy
Liaison, Athens, Greece

Ms. Rosa Maria Marti, Museu Textil i de la Indumentaria,
Barcelona, Spain

Mr. Kostas Messas, Research Assistant & Liaison, Greece

Mr. Manolo, Patronat Municipal De Turismo, Spain

Ms. Zumrat Nalsya Sube Marura, Department Minister of
Culture, Ankara, Turkey

Ms. Valentine Mort, Research Assistant and Liaison to Italy,
Penrose, Colorado, U.S.A.

Ms. Nellie O'Cleirigh, Irish Lace Historian, Dublin, Ireland

Mr. Michael O'Connell, Pro Media, Dublin, Ireland

Sr. Oliver, Presentation Covent, Youghal,
County Cork, Ireland

Mr. Jim and Ms. Mary Power, Research Assistants and
Liaison, Youghal, County Cork, Ireland

Ms. Judith Prendergast, National Portrait Gallery,
London, England

Mr. Branko Radivojevic, Director, Museum of Anthropology,
Thojrasski Musej, Belgrade, Yugoslavia

Mr. Milan Relic, Research Assistant and Liaison to
Yugoslavia, Zagreb, Yugoslavia

Ms. Taciser Onuk, Modern Crochet Designer, Turkey

Mr. Phillip Saran, Research and Location Guide,
Ankara, Turkey

Mr. Steven Saran, Research and Location Guide, Ankara, Turkey

Ms. Semra Sander, Turkish Radio and Television
Corporation, Ankara, Turkey

Mr. John Randolph Sauer, Project Executive Director, Dallas,
Texas, U.S.A.

Ms. Isabelle Sinden, Victoria and Albert Museum, London, England

Mr. Ronald Vick and Ms. Ulker Smith, Liaison Officer,
Ankara, Turkey

Ms. Maria Sudo, Research Assistant and Liaison, Spain,
Florence, Colorado, U.S.A.

Ms. Eleanor McD. Thompson, Winterthur Museum,
Delaware, U.S.A.

Ms. Pauline Turner, Modern Crochet Designer, England

Mr. Stephen H. Van Dyk, Cooper-Hewitt Museum, New York,
New York, U.S.A.

Mr. D. Ramon Estany Volart, Presidente de Volart
Encajes y Tejidos, S.A. Barcelona, Spain

Ms. Donna Walters, Research Assistant, Dallas, Texas, U.S.A.

Mr. James Walters, Modern Crochet Designer, England

Mr. Petros Zafiris, Greek Exports Promotion Organization,
Athens, Greece

RESEARCH & PRODUCTION

Ms. Annie Louise Potter, Executive Producer, Big Sandy,
Texas, U.S.A.

Mr. John Randolph Sauer, Co-Executive Producer,
Dallas, Texas, U.S.A.

Dr. Deyrol E. Anderson, Ph.D., Director of Research and
Production, Professor of Mass Communications, University of
Southern Colorado, Pueblo, Colorado, U.S.A.

Ms. Shirley A. Jurjovec, Research Writer and Production
Coordinator, Canon City, Colorado, U.S.A.

Mr. Joseph H. Reed, Director of Engineering and Systems
Coordinator, Colorado Springs, Colorado, U.S.A.

Mr. Arn Christian Sauer, Production Assistant, Photographer
Dallas, Texas, U.S.A.

Ms. Erika E. Anderson, Research Assistant, Denver,
Colorado, U.S.A.

Mr. Viktor Budnik, Plate Photography, Los Angeles,
California, U.S.A.

Lidji Design, Inc., Publication Design, Dallas, Texas, U.S.A.

Mr. Scott Campbell, Photographer, Big Sandy, Texas, U.S.A.

An exciting journey is just ahead. It's a journey back through time. It's a mixture of bold adventure with quiet solitude. It's a memorable passage of both fact and fancy that will leaf through the fading pages of history, allow personal glimpses into the minds and hearts of people, and provide a new perspective on a very old and cherished form of individual expression. This is the History and Art of Crochet.

Crochet, the simple act of pulling one loop of thread, yarn, or other material through another, is a modern leisure time activity, the basis for a thriving movement in contemporary wearable art, a means through which people have been able to make a living, and a way to fashion clothing and all manner of beautiful articles for the home.

Crochet is a simple technique never dealing with more than one simple stitch at a time. It's a useful skill that has been applied by generation upon generation down through the pages of recorded history. Simple as it is to learn, it's a mystery as to why it has been one of the last needlecraft arts to be fully developed. It survives because it is fun to do. Varieties of what can be done are endless. The beautiful and durable articles made have become treasured heirlooms from the past, or created to recapture the spirit and values of the traditional home and all that means for our modern times.

Often called "Poor Man's Lace," or "Imitation Lace," crochet does not surface in the flow of recorded history as an art in its own right until very recently — the early part of the 19th-Century. Modern popularization of the art, however, does not mean that it was invented during these modern times. By most definitions, crochet emerged as a result of experimentation with needle and thread during the Renaissance Period in Italy and France and quickly spread to other countries such as Flanders (Belgium), England, Ireland, and America.

The popularization of crochet as we know it today, however, can be firmly fixed as a textile commodity and as a leisure art during the 1830s. It came to worldwide attention for a number of reasons that will be described later in our journey through the History and Art of Crochet.

The incredible truth is that fragments of evidence exist to show that many of the same kinds of stitches and the techniques used today to work a fabric were known and used eons ago. Perhaps because the techniques are so simple to learn and become almost automatic to perform, the art can be traced back to the very dawn of time — as old as mankind itself.

The history of crochet remains a mystery. For all that has been studied about it, searching the world for bits and pieces of the art, studying the archives of the world's most famous and prestigious collections for references to it, pouring over volumes of carefully-researched rare books, monographs, and journals, the mystery endures; veiled with the passage of time; the absence of written records; pieces once made have fallen into decay and unavailable for study. While such direct evidence exists only in a few fragments, the serious scholar carries the feeling that behind these rare remnants is a certainty that primitive people the world over knew of the art and passed its secrets on from father to son; from mother to daughter.

Good Morning, Mama; Halle. The Mother is wearing an Irish Crochet Lace Collar from the mid 1800s. Courtesy of Victoria and Albert Museum.

Lydia Crocheting in the Garden at Marly, Mary Cassatt. Depicts crochet during the late 1800s. Courtesy of the New York Metropolitan Museum.

Where did crochet come from?

There is a notable absence of early crochet pieces in museum collections around the world. An early reference contained in the "Letters Patent" as granted to the Mercers of France in the year 1653 describes the enrichment of all forms of braid and lace, including "au crochet, et au fuseau." This reference is but one of several contained in these mid-17th Century documents.

Beside pieces of crochet themselves, there is also an absence of ancient crochet hooks. There are, however, large collections of needles, bobbins, and pins. Why haven't crochet hooks survived along with these other tools? Did they even exist during primitive times? If so, in what form? How were they made to assist the human hand? How were they discarded after use? Why?

While paintings are often an excellent source of detailed information about clothing, styles, fashions, customs, and beliefs through the ages, there are no paintings available in the world's galleries that show recognizable crochet until the mid-1800s. Many writers on the subject have documented that crochet developed rapidly from the year 1830, and that by the 1850s had become an art form of its own. An exhibition of the arts in the year 1851 featured an award-winning dress made by an important figure in the art, Mlle. Eleonore Riego de la Branchardiere — a creative genius in her day who helped to nurture the art and the industry of crochet to its peak of excellence.

This award-winning dress represents one of the finest pieces of crochet art that has ever been produced. The pattern is elaborate and intricate.

A drawing from the book of Mlle. Riego de la Branchardiere of her award winning child's crochet lace frock. Gold Medal Winner at the Great Exhibition of 1851. Courtesy of the British National Library.

It served as an inspiration for many new crochet designs and innovations to come.

By 1853, the largest number of exhibitors in the Dublin Exhibition presenting their works in the lace category entered pieces of crochet. The incredible growth of crochet is well-documented from these times during the first half of the 19th Century. Patterns were widely distributed. A rising leisure class of people had more time to devote to the art. Its beauty and simple charm knew no class barriers.

While some crochet workers in Ireland during the 1800s produced crochet in order to sell their works and quite literally survive because of it, wealthier men and women of England and other countries found it a useful way to pass the time. In America, consistent with a way of life that was to span several generations, women used crochet to decorate their homes and even fashion complete garments with their newfound

"Fascinator": An American indoor cap from the 1870s. The long lappets are crocheted with cream wool in a shell pattern, and are threaded with pink satin ribbon. Courtesy of the New York Metropolitan Museum.

crochet skills. Men, women, and even children throughout the civilized world quickly learned and adapted their skills in the art of crochet — within the space of fifty short years — to create beauty and add artistic expression — to become part of the on-going mystery of crochet; its compelling interest; its popularity.

People of all ages quickly discovered for themselves the incredible flexibility and diversity of crochet. The art of crochet offered an enormous range of possibilities for both application and personal accomplishment.

Unlike other needlecraft forms, any mistake made while crocheting can be immediately corrected. A few simple stitches can be used in endless creative variations. One needs only a length of material, a hook, and hands. With practice, crocheting can become almost automatic and can be done anywhere. It has become a universal language. One avid crocheter meeting a total stranger observed to be crocheting can develop an immediate friendship and share ideas as well as cultural appreciation. The enjoyment of crochet as an experience is shared worldwide.

Furthermore, as compared to other textile crafts, crochet can be learned quickly and easily, even by small children. More than perhaps any other art form, crochet offers opportunity for experimentation with designs, variations of patterns, colors, textures, and fabric development.

With but a few learned stitches, such as the chain stitch, single crochet, and double crochet stitches, patterns and shapes can be easily done. Other stitches such as the slip, treble, and double treble, offer more possibilities. The basic and most fundamental stitch for all crochet work, however, is the chain or tambour stitch.

At times, fine threads and hooks are used to create delicate trimmings and decorative pieces. By using larger hooks and heavier materials, one can produce everything from bedspreads to winter sweaters and rugs.

Anyone familiar with the skills of crocheting has experienced the freedom that the art form offers. Its variety and flexibility challenge the imagination and there is quite literally no known boundary for what can be accomplished — with a simple hooked tool and a continuous strand of material. Crochet has been called "imitation" lace, but has quickly developed into an art in its own right. It can also be used to produce a knitted look. The appearance of patchwork or weaving can also be done in any number of patterns — limited only by the imagination of the artist.

In our journey through the past, we will pause to wonder at the incredible skills represented by individual samples of the crochet and lace-making arts. We will discover ancient techniques and a tradition of expression in these art forms that have spanned centuries of time — far earlier than the 19th Century — and we will discover how techniques of stitching passed down from one generation to another have been preserved, admired, and refined.

Through the work of individual craftsmanship, our journey will explore the beauty of that expression through the eyes and skilled hands of artists who lived many centuries ago. Through their art, we can see the beauty that they must have seen. We can feel the pain that some of them must have felt. We can appreciate the quiet pride that the workers of antiquity must have known as they developed what are today regarded as masterpieces of their art.

Art is personal. Individual. It reaches out to others. It tells the truth about life. It represents what artists, think, and are. Its expression is a special gift that reflects both perfection and sensitivity. It is a delicate balance of the intellect and emotion. It portrays life just as do the great arts of painting, sculpture, music, or literature. It is the mark of a creative person every bit as revealing as a signature or a handwritten letter. It expresses the mind and heart of the artist. But art is even more. It can be equally revealing about a culture — the collected traditions of an entire civilization; a way of life. Art may be produced by the skilled labors of the hand, yet it is capable of touching the soul.

Crochet is one such art. Each piece is the work of a sensitive spirit — thinking of making something special for a child, a dear friend, the home, or for oneself — a bit of beauty for its own sake. It pleases the spirit, warms the heart, and expresses affection.

Through the history and art of crochet, one can understand people better — their hopes, their dreams, their fears. Handicraft arts, great paintings, music, and masterpieces of literature are all reflections of character, thought, and life experiences. The arts of a people also bear testimony to cultural influences, the traditions they hold dear, and even their attitudes toward themselves. True art endures. It can be seen and admired through following generations. It has a life of its own and no one can look upon it without feeling the currents of emotion that were present in the artist when the work was first created.

The term "crochet" is a relatively modern name for very old needle-worked art. It comes from the French word "croc" or "croches," and from an older Danish word "krooke," which means hook. Known in Western Europe by the 16th Century, the technique of crochet can also be dated to earliest times of pre-history, depending upon how the art is defined.

Many other countries of the world have their own names for what we know as crochet, but the adaptation of the word from the French language has survived since it was first used.

The mystery persists. Where did crochet really come from? It is inadequate to merely suggest that "its beginnings are shrouded in mystery" — there are some answers available to the serious student of its history.

One answer to the beginnings of crochet can be found in the fact that its techniques can be found in many forms. There is not just one kind of work that can be properly called crochet. Expression of these variations in form can also be divided into other groups that are called by different names across countries or continents of the world. Crochet, as we know it today, developed out of

basically two forms: fabric and lace. But each of these forms had different beginnings.

Fabric, for example, has been made with wool and large hooks to make blankets, shawls, and clothing. In the literature of crochet, a most commonly-accepted story presents crochet as "shepherd's knitting."

The name is used to popularize the observation that shepherds gathered wool from their sheep, or the strands of wool that had become snagged in the bushes and thorns of their peasant pastures. By then spinning their wool strands, they were able to produce continuous strands of a dense type of material common to the making of heavy sweaters, caps, shawls, jackets, and socks, as well as blankets and coverings for windows to ward off the chill of evening in their humble homes.

Shepherd boy gathers sheep wool snagged on branches in a pasture.

Shepherd's knitting using wool has been based on variations of stitching known for hundreds, if not thousands of years. Workers counted their stitches, individually or in groups, and produced all manner of durable garments and decorations for the home. Thicker yarns required larger hooks. Slender hooks required finer threads.

A second form for the beginnings of crochet can be said to have developed from the art of lace-making where hooked needles have been used to produce both laces and embroideries. Made with fine threads and delicate hooks, crochet laces are a marked contrast to the "shepherd's knitting" approach.

Some early pieces of crochet lace are deliberate attempts to imitate bobbin laces or other needlepoint laces. Applying crochet techniques, delicate imitations of real lace could be produced much faster than traditional techniques of lace-making allowed. Some of the best crochet-lace pieces are said to have originated in Italy and Spain by the early 16th Century, where it was done by the nuns of many convents and churches sprinkled throughout the countryside. Called simply "nun's lace," this form of crochet used inexpensive materials, including mostly wool and cotton, to produce some exquisite vestments, holy cloths, and embroidered pieces for the church.

These two basic forms — fabric and lace — provide a backdrop against which the mystery of the early development of crochet can be examined. Evidence of these two forms of development is obvious since it is known that as early as 1812,

An early looping technique was used to create the Arizona Indian Cap and Legging during the 13th Century. Courtesy of the Peabody Museum, Harvard University.

a little book called "Memoirs of a Highland Lady," written by Elizabeth Grant, describes a visit to an old Uncle and Aunt at Inverdruie, Scotland, and the shepherd's knitting that was commonly known and done at the time.

"Sometimes when he was not well, he wore a plaid cloak and a nightcap, red or white, made by his industrious wife in a stitch she called shepherd's knitting. It was done

with a little hook, which she manufactured for herself out of a tooth of an old tortoiseshell comb, and she used to go on looping her homespun wool as quickly as fingers could move, making not only caps, but drawers and waistcoats for winter wear, for the old husband she took such care of."

Who taught such people these skills? Who experimented with ways to fashion their hooks? Were slivers of shell preferred over perhaps other possible materials available to them at the time? Was the technique known by many homemakers of each village, or were the skills possessed only by a favored few?

By 1845, it is documented that crochet laces were sold in Cork, Ireland through the Ursuline Convent in Black Rock. Most pieces made and sold were the products of children who attended the convent school.

As yet another example of fabric-making using crochet techniques, it is known that a Russian gentleman and late Czar once owned a pair of slippers that were made in a single pattern by his bride some thirty years before they were discovered in 1858.

These examples of fabric and lace forms of what can fairly be called "modern" crochet, are among the earliest known pieces of evidence available for study.

The modern "art" of crochet is generally agreed to be an innovation of the 1850s and is an outgrowth of both "shepherd's knitting" and "lace." The "history" of crochet in terms of technique, however, can be traced back across the reaches of time to some of the world's earliest and most ancient civilizations.

While the crochet hook as it is known today is conceded to be an invention of the 19th Century, the looping of decorative knots and the making of stitches from a single strand of fiber or thread in order to make artistic designs for the embellishment of clothing is a very old and respected handicraft skill.

To restrict crochet to a strictly modern Western European influence is to ignore the many hundreds of years during which the technique was developing in other countries such as Syria, Persia, Morocco, Turkey, Egypt, Scandinavia, Yugoslavia, and Greece. Indeed, most other countries of the civilized world including those bordering the whole of the Mediterranean, Adriatic, and Aegean sea regions have used crochet as an art form. In terms of history it is universal. Timeless.

Defined simply as producing a fabric with a continuous loop, the basic principles of "crochet" as we know the art today, can be recognized in line drawings and paintings on pottery shards dating back thousands of years on at least three continents. Documented evidence exists and will be described in detail as we progress on our journey through time, into the fascinating history of crochet.

Evidence of technique can also be seen in the woven baskets of ancient Indian tribes of North America, and found in the assembled arts of the Assyrians, Persians, and others who lived along the shores of the Mediterranean and Aegean Seas thousands of years ago.

The act of crocheting requires only the simplest of tools — a piece of wood, bone, or ivory with a hook cut into it at one end, or a needle, or just a finger. Strands of fibers from plants and simple looping or knotting techniques using such a hook would have been far easier to develop than more complicated knitting frames or looms for weaving. It is here that the heart of the mystery needs further investigation.

Often, when investigating ancient sources for the roots of crochet, different interpretations of words or even symbols that are used in written or illustrated works can make an enormous difference as to the meaning that one might place upon it. An inspection of ancient tools and actual stitches in the few samples of threadwork that are available for study can be the most revealing and perhaps the most accurate way to establish the art as well as the history of crochet.

The real basis of crochet, after all, is simply the act of pulling one loop through another from a length of material — even long strands of wild grasses growing in the fields. The hook itself was no doubt fashioned as a substitute for fingers that were simply too large and bulky to reach through a small loop in order to pick up another loop.

Must crochet always be done with a hooked needle? This is yet another question tied to the mystery.

The most ancient of all handicraft tools — the needle — was used by primitive people to sew

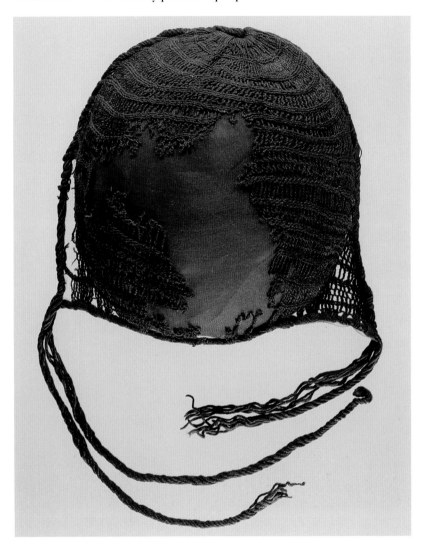

Bronze Age Hairnet found in a tomb in Denmark which clearly demonstrates the ancient looping technique. Courtesy of the Nationalmuseet, Denmark.

skins together for clothing, used with a looping technique for the ancient art of netting, and was common to all ancient cultures for basket-making and weaving. Needles have also been used since early times to help decorate fabrics and even accomplish primitive embroideries. Later, needles

Leather net cut from a single piece of leather and worn by sailors and soldiers as loincloth protection circa 1400 B.C. Courtesy of the British National Museum.

Net made from flaxen cord and used for fishing and bird catching circa 1250 B.C. Courtesy of the British National Museum.

Relief carving depicting the fringe trimming on the clothing of an Assyrian warrior circa 728 B.C. British National Museum.

were the essential tools for the making of lace and all kinds of other needlework.

In "The Ladies' Work-Table," published in 1850, it is noted that, "No one can look upon the needle without emotion; it is a constant companion throughout the pilgrimage of life."

Tracing the crochet-like technique back through history is difficult because very few examples are available for study. Like the tools which are not available for study, the materials used in the making of fabrics have disintegrated through time. Plant fibers, for example, known to have been used for the making of fabrics in ancient Greece and through the early Roman period have long since decayed and turned to dust. Pieces from the ancient Moorish Empire — known to have influenced the history of needle arts for at least 900 years, have been lost. Techniques for crocheting, unless worked in metals, have all but disappeared.

The earliest known uses of bronze in the Northern Regions of Asia Minor occurred by the year 3200 B.C., and the art of working with bronze was developed to its finest levels of craftsmanship by the ancient peoples of Mesopotamia where all manner of bronze ornaments and decorations were made and traded until about 1100 B.C.

During the "Bronze Age" of Scandinavia, a technique known as "sprang" was developed. Sprang is a process used to make a fabric by the manipulation of threads that are arranged parallel to each other on a warp which is fixed at both ends. Interlacing, intertwining, and interlinking are all forms of this type of thread manipulation. Sprang

fabrics result exclusively from the warp — the vertical threads.

The process happens row by row at one end of the warp. Because the warp is fixed at both ends, opposite movements of the threads appear at the same time at the opposite end of the warp. Therefore, the fabric is created top and bottom on the warp at the same time.

The fabric created starts at the upper end of the warp and another begins at the lower end of the warp. Eventually, the two halves meet in the middle. The design of the upper fabric is the exact mirror image of the fabric at the lower end. At the meeting point, some form of fastening is used to lock the contrary twisting from the ends into place, preventing the unraveling of the piece.

The resulting fabric has an elastic characteristic across the width as well as the length. This characteristic has made the sprang technique appropriate for making many different types of clothing. Long before the evolution of knitting, sprang was the quickest way to make stretch material. Variations in the technique have made sprang difficult to recognize, much less categorize. Each alteration of technique suggests regional differences or skills development in the making of fabric and other decorations.

In Borum Eshoi, Denmark, for example, an artifact dating back to the Scandinavian Bronze Age has been found and preserved in Denmark's National Museum in Copenhagen. It is a woman's hairnet that was made with continuous strands that were pulled and looped, possibly with a hook. Through carbon-dating techniques, the net is established as being produced in approximately the year 2748 B.C. Considered to be one of the oldest and most beautiful artifacts ever found in the northern regions, this priceless hairnet was sifted out of a grave near Aarhus, Denmark. It was made with great skill and the advanced technique uses multiple twist interlinkings and ridges. This hairnet, among other early Danish finds, may represent one of the only historical examples that can be considered as a "luxury" sprang fabric.

The hairnet came from a grave near the town of Borum Eshoi that was a mound some 120 feet across and twenty feet high. The expertise in both design and skill represented in this and other early Danish finds dating back to the Bronze Age lead some scholars to believe that these fabrics probably belonged to chiefs, or even royalty.

When discovered in 1871, the woman's hairnet was examined in great detail and was at that time, an unrecognized type of wearing apparel. A major clue that identified the piece as produced by the sprang technique was the two small discrepancies that appeared on either side of the central line. An exact copy of this hairnet was made and shown at the Paris World's Fair in 1889. This discovery led certain textile museums in Europe to re-evaluate specimens that had earlier been labeled as knitting, netting, or lace. After closer inspection, many such specimens were determined to be sprang.

Rediscovery of this technique also led to the belief that it was being practiced for centuries in various isolated communities. Sprang has been discovered in Croatia, Yugoslavia, Spain, Libya, Persia, Tunisia, Peru, Mexico, Guatemala, in Arizona of the Southwestern United States, and in many other areas of the civilized world. Where sprang exists today, it is done mainly for the purpose of making belts, a level of sophistication which is far below the sprang method used in creating the hairnet from Denmark and other ancient pieces.

In addition to Bronze Age evidence coming from the Scandinavian region, another important collection of documents can be found through the many existing records in the Cuneiform writings.

Cuneiform writings, preserved in both stone and clay tablets, have been carefully studied by scholars of antiquity for hundreds of years. Known for at least 3000 years, Cuneiform and Egyptian hieroglyphics recorded the human history of the Near East and offer the modern researcher a vast store of information.

Found throughout the Mesopotamian region, these tablets provide economic records, instructions for agriculture, the raising of crops, the intricacies of making textiles, and many other subjects of commercial interest at the time they were written. Further, they constitute a priceless treasure for all of us as a source for the study of literature through a period that spans across a 3000-year period of history.

Fine examples of fishing nets made of both leather and flax fibers from 1400 to 1250 B.C., can be studied in the British National Museum. Some of these nets, cut from single pieces of animal skin, or made from flaxen cords, were used in Thebes as well as other ancient cities. They demonstrate the patience with which early hunters and fishermen must have worked to produce them.

Trimmings and decorations for clothing made between 883 and 859 B.C., as represented by the flowing robes heavily embroidered and fringed with knotted edgings worn by the ancient Assyrian King, Ashurbanipal II, are also available for study in the British Museum. Beautifully preserved in stone, these ancient carvings, sculptured works, and relief drawings depict warriors decorated with embroidered clothing, garments fringed with pattern swirls, and articles fringed with tassels.

In the Benaki National Museum in Athens, Greece, an exceedingly rare sample is available for study that is called simply "threadwork" by the curators. It is from an excavation of a tomb in Egypt and is dated somewhere between 900 and 1100 A.D.

At first glance, it is like looking at one of our most modern and favorite crochet designs known as the "chevron." In this ancient piece, however, the use of chevrons in order to create a ripple pattern in the fabric is a very advanced form of the art and is identical to modern patterns used for making afghans. The chevron and ripple pattern are standard in the repertoire of most modern crocheters.

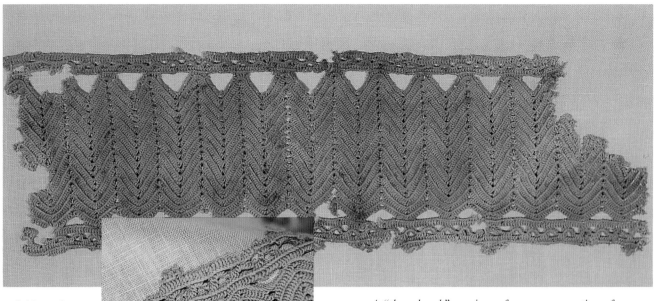

A close-up view of this ancient "threadwork" reveals stitches remarkably similar to crochet stitches.

A "threadwork" speciman from an excavation of an Egyptian tomb dated between 900 and 1100 A.D. The chevron design in this ancient garment edging or curtain piece represents an advanced needle technique. On display at the Benaki National Museum, in Athens.

A copy worked in crochet accurately duplicates this ancient "threadwork" specimen.

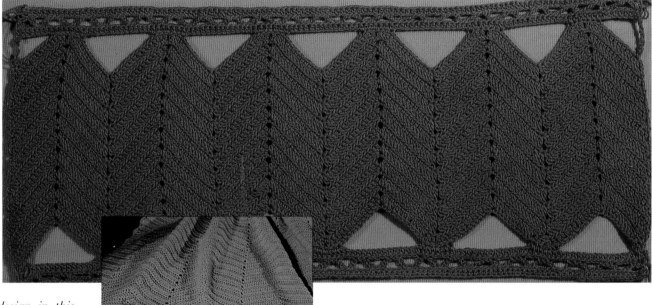

The ripple design in this contemporary crocheted afghan is virtually identical to the ripple design created in the ancient Egyptian "threadwork."

The Egyptian sample stands mute, but speaks to us across the generations. Most convincingly, the piece isn't a simple or crude pattern of chain stitches alone — a technique thought to have been invented sometime during the 1600s. It is an advanced style showing a definite pattern and skilled technique.

The sample cannot tell us whether or not it was made with a needle, but close inspection causes one to wonder how else it could possibly have been made. An implement of some sort would be required to produce such delicate and uniform stitching.

The best available information about this sample suggests that it was possibly an edging for a garment, or perhaps a piece of a curtain.

This important sample constitutes priceless evidence that "stitching in the air" was known long before the laces of the 1500s that most modern writers on the subject say was invented in the 16th Century and caused a major revolution of technique for the art of lace-making.

Historian and textile scholar Ms. Lila de Chaves, of Greece, has concluded that "interlacing with loops was used by the people of the Neolithic Age before the discovery of the spindlewheel, or the spinning-wheel, as far back as 5000 years B.C."

She adds that "...We refer to such pieces as 'knotless netting' because the fibers or threads are interlaced with each other and without the use of knots...identical to the techniques of knitting with the needle and crochet, which developed at an especially fast pace during the last four centuries in the countries of the Eastern Mediterranean and which rely on the method of interlacing with the help of a long, continuous thread for their construction." According to Ms. Chaves, the technique was very complex and slow to perform.

There are other ancient samples of work done with a needle during these early generations that also simulate knitting, netting, and crochet. So what's in a name? Does the absence of a recognized name mean that the art or technique did not exist? The mystery endures.

Ancient techniques of working with a needle have been called by many names throughout history — needle-coiling, knotless netting, cross-knit looping, looped needle-netting, vatsom, coptic knitting, and naalebinding.

In the ancient art of naalebinding, for example, the threads used are not tied in knots; rather, loops are interlaced. And, according to expert researchers, fingers were used to make the loops, and flat bone needles about five centimeters long were used to interlace loops. It is also known that ancient naalebinding was done with short lengths of thread, as opposed to long, continuous threads. It is generally agreed that naalebinding

Fragment of Naalebinding from excavations in Dura-Europos. Courtesy of Yale University Art Gallery.

was a prelude to needlepoint lace, interlacing, and a forerunner to knitting and crochet.

One of the most ancient samples of this technique came from Egypt between the 4th and 6th Centuries A.D. The sample is a short stocking. Samples of what appear to be a pair of coptic stockings are available for study in the Royal Ontario Museum of Toronto, Canada. They date back to "at least the 4th and 5th Centuries, B.C." Another sock using identical techniques for its construction is located in the Victoria and Albert Museum in London.

On close inspection, these "knitted" pieces of footwear appear to be done by ordinary knitting techniques. But there is a difference. Threads are twisted at every stitch using a technique capable of producing a true knitted structure.

It is the opinion of expert researchers that the working of material for such coptic knitted stockings was done with a needle of either bronze or bone — shaped much like a coarse darning needle — and represents an ancient art that is "an extension of a basic basketry or netting technique, which in its simplest form is a single loop worked through a single loop...a technique widely used since prehistoric times."

Author of an article on Textile History for the Royal Ontario Museum, Ms. Dorothy K. Burnham, has documented these findings and her research concludes that:

". . .a distinction must be made between single thread techniques like true knitting and crochet that are done with a comparatively unlimited length of yarn and the various forms of single-needle knitting, where only a short length is used. These are certainly primitive and seem to date back to the earliest attempts at textile manufacture."

Similar techniques can be seen in head coverings of Arab origin that were found during the excavation at Anbtinopolis from the 2nd Century, A.D. These samples are now located in the Staatl National Museum in Berlin.

There are other primitive textiles in the collections of other world-famous museums that come from these same periods in history. Many fine examples can be found of hair strainers made with these same special techniques. Hair strainers were common in early times because many household items had to be strained before they could be put to use in the common peasant household. Milk was strained to eliminate cow hair and leaves. Ale was strained to separate mash and hops. One of the most common strainers was a wooden cup with holes in the bottom and a piece of coarse textile made with hair.

Examples of hair strainers that were made with the naalebinding technique, a Danish term that means "needle-binding," can be found in Scandinavian countries.

Anthropologists commonly call this technique "knotless netting." It is a technique evident in garments that protected hands and feet in cold weather. Knotless netting also appears in a variety of other cultures throughout the world during the Bronze and Iron Ages.

Unlike knitting and crochet, knotless netting does not rely on a continuous thread. Instead, it was done with pieces of thread less than a yard or two in length and required continual joining of threads. Mysteriously, the joining of the threads is not accomplished with a simple knot, but by a method of spinning, or twisting of threads together.

Coptic knitting, another term for the looping technique is said to date back to between the 4th and 7th Centuries, B.C. One 7th Century piece is a hairnet found at Fayoum, Egypt. Other tombs at Antinoe contained rare Egyptian dresses, robes, and other kinds of head coverings dating to the 6th Century, B.C. Each piece demonstrates a nearly identical "coptic" style — using knotted meshwork, circular patterns, and fringe trimmings with pulled and looped techniques.

Skills for the textile arts, particularly in ancient times, were rarely written out and distributed. Instructions were only passed down from one skilled person to the next — a mother to daughter, father to son, or communal teacher to small groups — generation after generation. History therefore contains many gaps across time as to the record of these skills. The few available samples must speak for themselves.

The mystery deepens when considering the fact that early needlework arts are known to have been widely-used and developed among people of different cultures who could not possibly have been together to talk about them, or share their secrets of technique.

While most of the existing records and interests in the ancient textile arts center on the regions of Western Europe and what was earlier known as Asia Minor, these same arts can be found on other continents. Each country of the world has its own history of the needlecrafts. Taken together, these distant lands represent a rich treasure of cultural heritage that is unique to each of them, yet in many ways, common to all.

From the tiny villages in the high Andes Mountains of Peru to the Steppes of Ancient China, and from the island communities of the Pacific to the Americas, the same basic techniques for netting, knitting, weaving, crocheting, and embroidering can be found. Why? How did their secrets travel across towering mountains and oceans? Who were the teachers? The mystery persists.

Were hooked instruments used to fashion these nearly identical garments? Were those implements of bone, metal, and wood similar to modern crochet hooks? How were their intricate designs, patterns, and motifs done, if not with some sort of tool when fingers alone could not possibly have done such work?

Exotic ceremonial costumes with crochet-like ornamentation, decorative trimmings for arms, ankles, and wrists, were fashioned during these early centuries out of both plant and animal fibers. Patterns and designs are truly unique and amazingly similar across continents — from those of pre-Columbian times in South America to the Bronze and Iron Ages of Europe.

Just as coptic knitting techniques found in Egypt are amazingly similar to those of modern crochet, Soumak artisans of South America are thought to have used a hooked tool to make the chain stitches that are identical in appearance to crochet stitches.

Time. Curiosity. Need. A desire to beautify. A basic human drive: to create! All of these elements of mind and spirit working together — for whatever immediate purpose — will inevitably lead to experimenting with something new — to discover and then refine — to see and to domesticate them.

The needle itself is a fundamental step in the development of handicraft arts. Known since the earliest Bronze Age, crude needles of various sizes, shapes, and dimensions are known to have been made for the working of fibers, hemp, flax, wool, and other more costly metals that have included gold and silver strands. Examples of ancient needles have been found in excavations in both Egypt and ancient Greece and are preserved in such world-famous museums as the Hamiltonia, the Pompeii, the British National Museum, and in the Benaki Museum in Athens.

The simple sewing needle is a forerunner of many needlecrafts, including crochet. Depending upon the technique employed, the needle has often given way to other tools such as shuttles, knitting needles, or crochet hooks as time and skills progressed.

Modern crochet — the art of using a hooked needle to pull loops from a continuous thread or fiber and working with but one stitch at a time — is closely related to other handicraft arts in the family of textiles. Crochet is most closely related to the arts of netting, knitting, tambour, and lace-making. All depend upon needles and most have used hooked needles at one time or another to produce or embellish a fabric by using looping and knotting techniques — one stitch at a time — with open spaces in between stitches. All but the most intricate refinements of lace-making represent arts that have been practiced in one form or another since very early times.

The history of crochet is inseparable from the history of many other similar crafts that include netting, knitting, Tunisian crochet, tambour, and other needle laces. Through the ages, these forms of the needlecraft arts have evolved their own distinct sets of techniques, styles, fashions, and utilitarian values. But, as each form of the art advanced, so have the variations of design which today set them apart — one from the other.

All of these basic handicraft arts have shared, borrowed, and adapted many of the same tools — the needle, hook, frame, backgrounds of networked fabrics, and often the same raw materials such as flax, wool, cotton, silk, and even strands of gold and silver. Each art form has made its own contribution to the needs and artistic tastes of people throughout the civilized world. Each has spawned worldwide textile industries. Each has come into its own as a separate branch of artistic achievement. Each is known to have influenced the other. Each has its own history of advantages as well as its own limitations. Each has long held a distinctive purpose and uniqueness. Each shares in the richness of its own historical traditions, yet each is seen to have built upon earlier forms of the handicraft arts. Together they form a tapestry of history that is interwoven through many cultures and across many thousands of years.

In his book, "The Sacred History of Knitting," Heinz Edgar Kiewe compared knitting needles, crochet hooks, and other implements for the textile arts with those of biblical times where clothing was woven from continuous strands, or done by the stitching of loops. He concluded that the history of these ancient arts of crochet, knitting, netting, weaving, twisting, and braiding are so closely related that they are inseparable.

One way to investigate the techniques of related ancient handicraft arts is to examine the implements that were used to create and decorate fabric. Related techniques become one large family through the tools they employ and some of these tools survive today as testimony to the ingenious nature of mankind.

When one looks at the tools that were used, the art and history of each handicraft can be better and more accurately seen. There are similarities and differences among the various tools that characterize each art form. Each tool was developed to solve immediate problems, or to develop yet another style or technique. This adaptation and development produced new shapes, textures, and dimensions.

In fact, the tools themselves have not changed much in thousands of years. A knitting needle, a weaver's shuttle, a crochet hook, a sewing needle, or a tambour hook found in a modern sewing basket are essentially unchanged from those of distant times when they were first fashioned out of bone, bronze, or wood.

It is the similarity between the tools that are used in all of the textile handicraft arts and not their differences that draw all of them together. Hooking, looping, crossing, braiding, and interweaving are common to them all. Purpose and application are where the differences develop.

An in-depth investigation of the techniques of related ancient handicraft arts must also

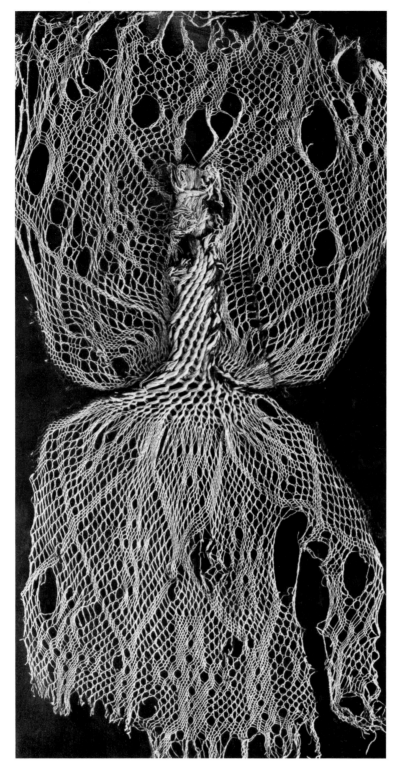

Ancient sprang sample from Egypt. Courtesy of the Victoria and Albert Museum.

communal workers depending entirely upon the skills of their hands to earn a living, crochet and related art forms gradually became the pride of nations — the stuff of dreams — the means for both survival and prosperity.

Stitches for design. Appropriate tools for the working of materials. Spinning continuous threads for production. Building toward a future and sharing knowledge. All of these elements are inherently part of the art and history of crochet and its related techniques. A brief look at each related technique will help to set a context for crochet itself as one of the most ancient and important forms or branches of ageless traditions.

One major technique closely related to crochet is a type of knotting and looping known as "netting." The technique dates back thousands of years and is considered to be one of the oldest of all techniques of lace-making. There are actual museum samples that are at least 3000 years old. Netting was often the technique used for making fishing and bird catching implements.

Beyond the crude attempts of primitives to fashion nets of knotted strands for fishing or for the snaring of small animals, netting as a handicraft art to make and embellish clothing is known to have at least a 4000- year history.

Burial gowns found in Egypt, particularly in the excavations at Thebes, demonstrate an astonishing skill with interwoven net work. Pliny the Elder, a Roman scholar, wrote in 52 A.D., "...these ancient Egyptian nets made to adorn and beautify, are so delicate that they would pass through a man's ring, and a single person could

include the study of the ancient specimens, tracing their patterns back through various cultures and the influences of separate civilizations.

Under the refining influences of culture and a spreading civilization, handicrafts such as netting, knitting, tambour, and crochet were raised from "folk art" status to the level of professional.

Once known only as skills of necessity for the fishermen working their nets a few miles offshore, or of the shepherds who turned their fleeces into warm and decorative clothing, to the

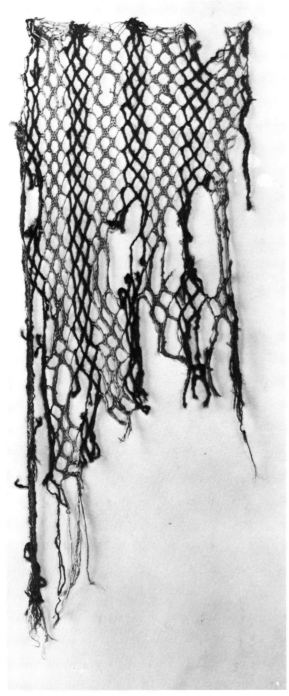

Ancient netting sample from Egypt. Courtesy of the Victoria and Albert Museum.

King of Egypt, whose threads are composed each of three hundred and sixty-five fibers; and in proof of the truth of this, Mutianus, who was thrice consul, lately affirmed at Rome, that he had examined it... and another corslet presented by the same King to the Lacedaemonians was closely inspected. It was of linen, ornamented with numerous figures worked in gold and cotton. Each thread is worthy of admiration, for though very fine, every one was composed of three hundred and sixty other threads, all distinct; the quality being similar to that dedicated to Minerva at Lindus."

M. Passalacqua, Egyptian Antiquities Museum, Montbijou, Berlin

From the studies of antiquities in ancient Egypt, to the Northern reaches of the "Steppes" of Mysia in Asia Minor, from discoveries in Peru and the ancient Mayan Huastecs of Central America; and from the European Middle Ages to all of the civilized regions of the world, netting has provided a satisfying means of expression in the handicraft arts for well over 3,000 years.

From Catherine de Medici, whose taste in fine laces was known the world over, and whose bed was covered with decorated net work, to Martha Washington, who delighted in making fashionable netting for the "trimming of dresses, curtains, caps, shawls, collars, tuckers, and ruffles," the arts of netting have captured the hearts of people the world over for generations. Rare, beautiful ornamentation has been made with mesh-sticks and netting needles — for antimacassars, counterpanes, and tamboured embroideries.

Netting is truly a distinct art of its own and forms a broad and interesting avenue for both research and appreciation back through time. The tools it employs are closely related to the refinements of both lace-making and crochet. It used needle shuttles and other implements to fashion knotted strands of fibers.

Knitting, another important related technique, can be traced to the 4th and 5th Centuries, A.D. A number of historians speculate that the art

carry a sufficient number of them to surround a whole wood."

Egyptian netting used flax strings composed of between 150 and 350 individual fibers. These delicate strands were "often ornamented with gold figures of animals, flowers, and intricate raised embellishments to enhance and glorify the wearer." These words describing a collection of Egyptian antiquities held in a museum in Montbijou, Berlin, Germany claim that ancient netting skills "far surpass those of modern times."

"In the Temple of Minerva, there are the remains of a linen corslet, presented by Amasis, form was known in much earlier times in many different forms. Apparently, the development of knitting was slow because weaving was already so widespread. The steel rods used in knitting required a high degree of skill to produce. In fact, metal rods were easily produced only after the art

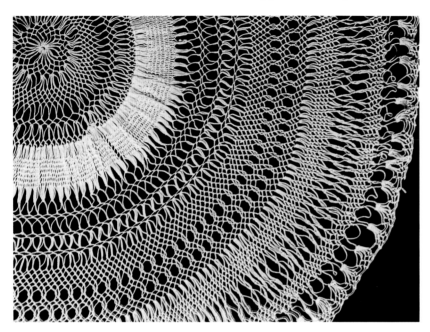

Modern netting still reflects the design of the ancient net.

of drawing steel through perforated plates was perfected during the reign of Queen Elizabeth I.

Also, no ancient Greek word for knitting can be found. Not until the Renaissance do words meaning "to knit" make an appearance. For example, the French word "tricot" appeared in 1616. Words for knitting in Germany, Spain, Italy, and Scandinavia came from the same time period. Arabia, where knitting supposedly originated, has no word exclusively dedicated to knitting. Hayyah is used to refer to the technique, but this same word also refers to weaving. Not until the end of the 15th century did the English word, knit, refer to making a fabric by tying, joining, gathering, or knotting.

The linkage between what we now identify as knitting and crochet rests, in part, on the fact that both techniques relied upon hooked needles for working small loops of material and that both work with a loop of material instead of its end.

Examples of three-dimensional, multi-colored articles of clothing made with knitted loops and pulled stitches have been found from the Pre-Columbian Age (2000 B.C. to 1000 A.D.) in Peru. Stockings, sweaters, shawls, and other examples are cited as being derived from the same techniques that ancient peoples in many parts of the world used in the making of baskets.

From a study of the tools and implements used by primitive peoples, knitting needles made of bone and bronze that appear to have no other useful purpose, confirm that the art is extremely old — using the simplest form of knitting, that of working a single loop through a single loop.

By modern definitions, knitting employs a continuous length of material worked with needles. However, with naalebinding, the earlier, simplest version of the technique, short lengths of grasses, reeds, animal sinews, lengths of fur, wool, and other materials were used. There are the scattered fragments of primitive specimens that exist in a handful of museums around the world, such as three fragments from Dura-Europos dated 256 A.D. It is clear that these short stems from plants or limited lengths of animal fur were twisted, and spliced together in order to make longer lengths for working into fabrics — an early form of spinning.

Naalebinding can also be used to produce a true knitted structure, but by a different method. Some creative ancient artisan must have discovered that new loops could be pulled through with a hooked needle. This was apparently the beginning of hand knitting with a hooked needle. This type of knitting needle is still commonly used in Egyptian villages.

Another example was presented by Walter Edmund Roth, in his "An Introductory Study of the Arts and Crafts and Customs of the Guiana Indians." He described a 1916 visit to the descendants of these Indians when he tracked the history of the ancient knitting technique. He was able to describe in detail the development of yarn crafts including knitting and even true crochet.

Hooked knitting needles are used even today for fabric construction in many villages sprinkled throughout the world. The work performed is often characterized by a tubular appearance in style, that is begun at the toe in socks, for example, and continued in widening rows to make ankle-length or longer footwear. The same techniques can be identified in the making of garment sleeves, caps, mittens, and other articles of clothing. Of interest to the history of knitting is also the fact that metals were also used as materials in the Byzantine world, by Vikings of the Northern provinces, in Scotland, Tibet, India, the Yemen, and in Greece hundreds of years before Christ. Metal wires, strands of gold, silver, and copper were laboriously intertwined into knitted structures, a separate art-form known as Trichinopoly, named for a village near Madras, South India called Tiruchirapalli. One of the oldest datable samples is from a grave of a 2nd Century woman in Southern Holland.

Cotton, wool, and silk, however, have been the favored materials for knitting throughout recorded history. Of interest too, is the fact that woolen socks, stockings, caps, and scarves, are clearly the most often produced products of hand-knitting, from earliest times until the middle of the 20th Century, if not to the present day.

Some of the most interesting sources for the history of knitting can be found in that region of the world dominated by Islamic cultural influences — from the Adriatic to China, and from Ankara and Istanbul in Turkey, to sections of North Africa. Using multi-colored fabrics, the use of four to five needles, designs, and motifs done as rosettes, stars, twists, and curlicues, are consistent styles of embellishment. Working in both flat and raised twists, the work produced by hand-knitted grid techniques is beautiful, durable, and a centuries-old tradition.

Combining the arts of crochet and knitting, Yugoslavians, Romanians, and the Greeks often prefer their own traditions of knitting with up to five short needles that are hooked on one end. Some parts of their works are knitted, but other parts incorporate standard techniques of crochet. The results are striking. Heavily ornamented, using ten to fifteen different colors, producing narrow patterns of coordinated geometric shapes, the variety of fabrics produced are unique, intricate, and often embroidered with silver braids and cords.

So unique are the styles produced in these various regions, that a wearer of stockings, for example, can be associated with a particular community and establish that person's social stand-

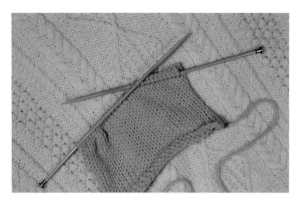

Modern sample of knitting representing an art handed down from primitive people the world over.

ing. At times, messages and coded requests have been woven into the fabrics to express spiritual beliefs, or to shield the wearer against evil. Intricate patterns are rich with symbolism and they therefore often contain value going far beyond the mere utilitarian.

In Russia, the story of knitting dates back to at least the 1100s, A.D. , and fine examples of the art can be found in the Metropolitan Museums of both Moscow and Leningrad. Their hand-knitted woolen socks, exquisite sashes, shawls, and knitted silk gloves are heavily ornamented with an astonishing variety of edgings, tassels, and embroideries. The art has flourished for centuries as an uncomplicated, household tradition.

Volumes have been written about knitting as an activity for both men and women throughout Western Europe. William Kennedy, in his "Annals of Aberdeen," commented that, "The spinning of wool and the knitting of stockings were regarded more as a species of amusement than as a laborious employment, and gave little interruption to their ordinary avocations." As a useful and

Modern Tunisian Crochet Hook.

practical craft, the ever-present knitting basket provided a means of passing the hours, occupying the mind, and producing something needed by every member of the household— warm socks, mittens, and mufflers against the chill of evening.

Francis Trochu, in his "The Cure d'Ars," wrote that he and his little sister Marguerite, "went out every day to graze the family donkey, cows, and sheep, taking our knitting with us as it was our custom to make stockings and other bits of clothing while looking after our animals."

In the works of poet William Cowper, a 19th Century English writer, we find an apt description for the occupation of knitting:

"...Her constant employment is knitting stockings and has not for many years worn any other than those of her own manufacture. She sits knitting on one side of the table, in her spectacles, and he on the other, reading to her, in his.

Yesterday, an old man came hither on foot from Kimbolton. He brought a basket containing two pair of bottle-strands, her own manufacture; a knitting bag, and a piece of plum cake."

Most museums are delighted to have even a few knitting specimens dating from 1200 to 1500 in their collections. A convent in Spain has a cushion dated 1275, and knitting is evidenced in Northern Italy before 1350 in a painting called "Knitting Madonnas" by Lorenzetti. There are other fine pieces in Switzerland that date from the 14th Century.

Knitting — common, ordinary, and without pretensions is the work of dedicated hands for family and household needs. Made with large measures of love, knitted fabrics as articles of clothing have always been practical as well as beautiful; an expression of nurturing care as well as demonstrations of skill. Reverend William Lee, of Calverton, England — a small village in the heart of the Sherwood Forest — is credited with being the first to take a mechanical or scientific interest in knitting. He invented a knitting frame in the mid 1590s that greatly increased the speed through which knitted fabrics could be manufactured. His frames were to become the primary tool used by quite literally thousands of busy knitters and created a "cottage industry" not only for England but throughout the continent that was to last for nearly 250 years.

Lee's frames were also a basis for the design of the circular knitting machines that were created during the early years of the Industrial Revolution in both England and the United States — machines that used his "bearded needle" and "floating loop" ideas that historians agree were largely responsible for automating the knitting process for the first time.

In the space of fifty short years, his simple knitting frame ideas that had once sparked a growing and profitable "cottage industry," were transformed into power-driven machines that gave a new and vigorous momentum to the burgeoning textile industries of two continents.

Through the centuries, national fashions in hand-knitted fabrics were to become increasingly ornate and distinctive. New imaginative designs worked with the simplest of hand-knitting tools led to innovations that quite literally established national standards — from country to country. Another related technique and form of crochet we now call "Tunisian" represents a sharing of techniques between the ancient skills of knitting and the modern art of crochet. There is evidence that the Tunisian Crochet form is a more recent development than knitting.

Tunisian Crochet, practiced for centuries in the Middle East, Northern, and Central Africa, is a distinct form of the crochet art that represents a bridging of not only technique, but cultural influence.

Sometimes called "Afghan" crochet, the roots of Tunisian technique and style are traced back to at least medieval times in Europe and historians agree that the art form made its way into Western Civilization through way of both Africa and Asia Minor.

To quickly fashion warm clothing, ancient sailors and shepherds alike are known to have made the tools they needed to work fibers, hemp, strands of slender reeds, and wool into the garments they wore.

Tunisian Technique uses a long hook resembling a knitting needle, but which has a hook carved into one end and a raised lip or ball at the other to keep the worked material from coming off the end of the hook.

Early craftsmen and women using the Tunsian Hook made their clothing and accesories with only the simplest of stitches.

The methods of Tunisian Crochet are a combination of knitting and crochet — a style that is extremely old in origin. It is commonly thought that the earliest knitting needles had hooks at the ends of them to better facilitate catching a loop of material and drawing it through itself to form another loop which forms rows of stitches.

Tunisian Crochet properly belongs to an ancient category of crochet sometimes known as "Shepherd's Knitting," or "Wool Crochet." Fabrics produced using this method are firm, contain rich textures, and are often embellished with surface motifs that are added after the basic garment has been produced.

Longer needles hold many more loops or stitches than do the shorter, standard crochet hooks. Often working with heavier materials, and sometimes combining or working with several strands simultaneously, the Tunisian Crochet offers an infinite variety of shapes, stitch patterns, and dimensions.

Modern sample of Tunisian Crochet by Pauline Turner, England.

Long, cylindrical needles for the holding of one or many stitches and containing a hook on one end and a cap or carved ball on the other, were used in the early history of this important textile handicraft. Later transported to Western Europe by Arab traders, these hooked needles seemed cumbersome and useless to Western eyes at first. An idea of what they should be instead of what they were, apparently caused some craftsmen to straighten them out, whittle their hooks off, and use them as knitting needles or "spits" as they are still used in France, many other countries of Western Europe, and in the Americas today.

More recently, Tunisian Crochet has been often called simply the "Afghan Stitch," or the "Tricot Stitch," as it made its way through the countries of Western Europe but most notably France.

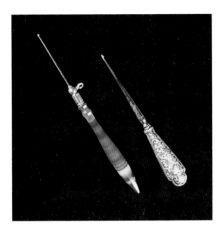

The Tambour hook and the Crochet hook are almost identical in design.

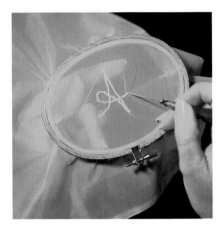

Tambour was worked on a fabric stretched over a hoop.

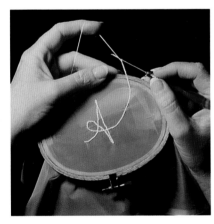

The Tambour technique possibly led to Crochet when someone just kept tambouring off the edge of the hoop, creating "stitches in the air."

But, called today by many names, the basic art-form can be found in every corner of the globe — from remote villages of Peru and other countries of South America, to China, Turkey, Yugoslavia, Greece, Italy, and Spain, as well as to the metropolitan centers of the United States.

Tunisian Crochet has traveled the world. Samples can be found in virtually every country and use a broad range of materials. At times extremely fine yarns and the narrowest of hooks are used to make a fabric that is open and has a "lace-like" pattern. At other times, the technique is found using heavier, thicker yarns and broadly-shaped needles to produce a tighter, denser fabric.

Depending upon need, the Tunisian style reflects extreme characteristics of adaptability and flexibility. Colors can be changed to imitate pictures. Layered effects are easily achieved by adding top-stitched motifs to a basic piece. Depending upon the purpose at hand, a worker can produce a heavy cloak for bracing against the severest of winter winds, or an intricate, multi-colored handbag to serve as a fashionable accessory for an evening on the town.

Crocheted panels embroidered with cross stitches, an effect that closely resembles weaving, can produce garments, rugs, window coverings, bedding, and all manner of decorative pieces quickly and easily. Working with both texture and color, the "Afghan Stitch" or "Tunisian Crochet" style offers a sense of freedom and creativity to the handicraft worker.

Many modern crochet designers enjoy working with this "Tunisian Style" and the opportunities it contains for flair, richness of texture, and eye-catching variety.

Tambour is the closest to crochet of all the related techniques, and probably most directly influenced the development and spread of the crochet laces. Tambour, based on the simple chain stitch, is of Far Eastern origin — China, Turkey, India, North Africa, and Persia. It was established in Europe by the middle of the 18th Century. Modern crochet and tambour share the same general technique of using a hooked needle to make loops out of a continuous piece of thread.

As a species of embroidery, yet one that bridges needlework and crochet, tambouring uses a hooked tool shaped much like a crochet hook but one that tapers to a hooked tip forming a small stiletto-type needle.

It is used to make chain stitches on top of fabric that is stretched. The very word "tambour" is a French word meaning "drum" and it aptly describes its fundamental technique — stretching a basic material across a frame much like a drum and working a design into it with a hooked needle and threads. The design is first sketched on a background material and then placed in a frame. Most commonly, two interlocking hoops are used to hold a background piece of material, mostly woven muslin in the early days. Then a small and often very fine crochet-type hook works the chain stitch onto the fabric from the thread which is held under the frame.

Later, machine-made net was used in place of the woven muslin. Using continuous chain stitches, light threads in a rainbow of brilliant colors, intricate motifs can be worked in cotton, cambric, crepe, satins, linens, and muslin to produce beautiful effects.

The hooks used to create the chain stitch have been made of ivory, bone, wood, and more lately, steel. Intricately carved, these "tambour hooks" were considered to be "needles" until the 20th Century, but they represent a unique tradition and heritage for quality of workmanship in the needlecraft arts for hundreds of generations.

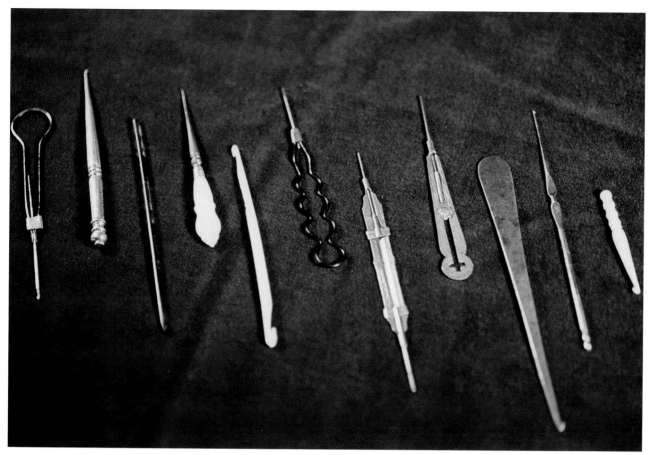

Selection of Antique Crochet Hooks. From the Author's personal collection.

Most tambour hooks are made so that a number of differently sized hooks can be fitted into a single handle. According to design and creative needs, a worker can select an appropriate tambour needle and clamp it into the same holder.

Tambouring as a separate art form, yet one that is tied directly to virtually all other branches of the needle arts, rose to its highest levels of perfection in Western Europe in the ecclesiastical context: church vestments, altar cloth embellishments, robes, adornments for sacred books, tapestries, and edifices.

Developing from the Far East and embracing the Saracenic influence as well as that of the Byzantine empire of the Middle East, the most delicate and exquisite pieces of art were created in the protected niche of church handicraft history and are known as "Opus Angelicum." Capes and semi-circular mantles worn by bishops and other religious leaders were often embroidered by nuns in scores of convents sprinkled throughout Western Europe and rank as some of the most magnificent garments owned by the Church.

Based on this simple and almost universal "chain" stitch technique, many other examples of the early tambour can be found in vestments, altar cloths, and alb flounces, carefully preserved by the Church. Tucked away in the treasure rooms of cathedrals and displayed only on special Holy Days and other ceremonies, these priceless pieces of tambour were often worked on old hand knotted net ground.

Ancient Tambour and Modern Crochet are techniques related so closely in nature that perhaps, in their simple forms, they are only separated by the fact that Tambour is secured on a ground fabric and Crochet does not need a supporting ground fabric. Crochet probably developed from tambour or embroidery in chain stitches done with a small hook. It was an easy transition from tambouring with a hook to dropping the ground material entirely and creating a decoration with a series of linked chains or loops to produce "crochet stitches in the air."

Crochet and all its related techniques rely upon continuous fibers or materials and the use of

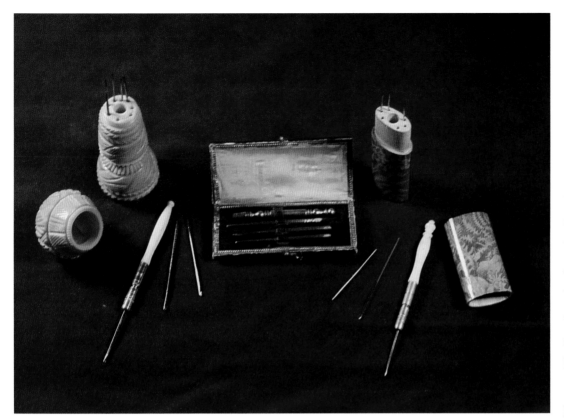

Selection of Antique Crochet Hooks. From the Author's personal collection.

hand-held hooks, needles, and shuttles. To produce long or continuous threads, the preliminary step of spinning becomes an art unto itself that is necessary for all of the handicraft skills. Any treatment of the histories of these related techniques must therefore include spinning. The fact that spinning is as ancient as any of these arts is an important confirmation that the arts existed and have been practiced over at least the past 6,000 years.

Attributed in legend to Minerva, spinning is the act of twisting a number of small threads together — from flax, wool, or other fibers — and forming them into a long and unbroken line of material. In primitive times, spinning was done completely by hand with the use of spindles. Wheels of wood and later of iron were among early inventions to speed up and refine the process.

Spinning "jennies," "mules," "water frames," and other innovations were made on the basic spinning wheel over the years, but the basic techniques have remained the same throughout the history of the art.

The exploration of crochet and its related techniques also reveals that flax — one of the oldest agricultural crops produced — is marked as the most ancient of all materials expressly grown for the purpose of spinning. Examples of flax cloth can be dated to thousands of years ago in the primitive provinces of Stone Age Switzerland and to at least 4,000 years ago in Egypt. The silkworm is also a heavy contributor to the ancient as well as the modern textile arts. This tiny "Bombyxmori" spins its cocoon and produces the strongest, finest, and most beautiful threads known.

Nearly 3,000 years before Christ, the silkworm was bred in the great empires of the Far East and throughout the Orient. It was considered a national treasure and a closely-guarded secret for generations. Through six major Dynasties of China, anyone caught giving away the silkworm secret for the making of fine threads was tried, publicly disgraced, and executed. In fact, there are many stories of attempted smuggling in China spanning a sweep of history covering more than 3,000 years.

It is recorded that two Christian missionaries, who were in China at the time from their native homeland of Persia, were responsible for hiding silkworm eggs in their hollow canes as they boarded ship for their home church in Constantinople. Managing to pass through frequent and most rigorous inspections safely, they were able to return home and breed their own silkworms to produce silk in Turkey, Anatolia, and other parts of Asia Minor. This theft of the Chinese national treasure introduced silk to the Western world for the first time.

Cotton, on the other hand, was easily produced and was the staple for textile-making among commoners since at least 3000 B.C. It was called the "lamb plant" in many early cultures, or "karpas" in Greece, for "wool-bearing trees." It has remained as one of the most commonly used materials for spinning that the world has ever known.

A Greek historian, world traveler, and explorer of the 5th Century B.C., wrote of cotton: "The wild trees in India bear for their fruit a fleece surpassing that of sheep in beauty and quality and the natives clothe themselves in cloth therefrom using slender reeds held in the fingers to twist and pull their threads into articles for wearing..."

These and other fibers have been integrated into the construction of every major kind of textile down through the ages by another ancient artform, weaving. This process stands as testimony to the creative ingenuity of people the world over and is important because it formed a basis for later embellishments such as fringes, knotting and embroidery. It was also a basis for later techniques such as drawnwork and cutwork which were the forerunners to early lace.

Understanding the development and flow of the skills, techniques, and adaptation of the early laces will further unravel the mystery of the Art and History of Crochet. The early laces represent an array of techniques that bridge changing styles and incorporate cultural influences.

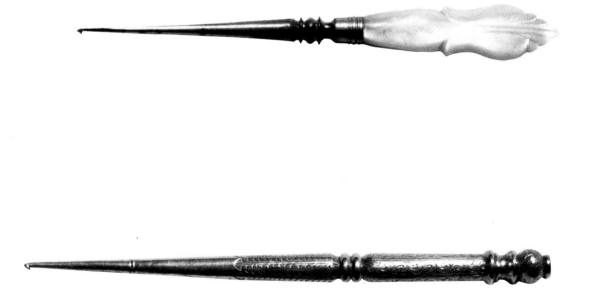

To fully appreciate the heritage that is shared with everyone interested in crochet, it is necessary to understand something of lace and lace-making. The uses of lace by royalty, courts, and officials of state the world over, had an enormous impact on the reasons why crochet became so popular by the 1830s and has remained so. In fact, crochet was originally developed for the purpose of imitating the more expensive and very time-consuming laces.

During the Middle Ages, great events swept through Western Europe that were to change the very existence of nations. Later, a rising middle class was developing strength. An Industrial Revolution was to catapult societies forward with giant leaps across three continents. The "Machine Age" replaced feudal empires and old aristocracies. Royalties of the past became figureheads and symbols stripped of their powers and their excesses. The "melting pot" of society brought by ever-increasing populations were making their demands for a share in the "good life" and position by virtue of birth alone was changing dramatically to a belief in individual worth.

All of these sweeping ideas — a revolution of mind — were to ignite a new kind of renaissance within the space of a few generations.

The study of lace and its development helps to explain these massive changes for societies throughout Western Europe and even for America.

Over the centuries, in most civilized countries on earth, many people have experimented with the arts of lace-making. Early history demonstrates clearly that those who produced it first were men; hunters and fishermen, fashioning these structures of knotted strands of fiber to trap animals or catch fish for food. Craftsmen all, whose skills and patience set them apart from the rest of the people in their villages.

Some of the earliest civilizations on earth are known to have constructed their snares and traps with woven fibers, cords, or strips of cloth. Shards of pottery made by these ancients hold primitive imprints as examples of their knowledge and demonstrate the techniques they used. Weighted nets for fishing are known to have been made as early as 2000 B.C. A few samples are still intact that establish both the mode and special purposes for the ancient art of netting that were used either as a matter of necessity for food gathering, or as personal ornamentation draped about their bodies. The finest pieces of their work were made with patient care and used only for special occasions such as important religious rites, celebrations, marriages, or funerals. Sometimes, heavier or lighter strands of different colored fibers were added to produce striking contrasts and dimensions.

The Kircheriano Museum in Rome holds a rare collection of ancient nets, ingeniously knotted game bags, and open-worked utensils made by using strands of coarse natural fibers. Looking at these ancient

Fishing nets are one of the earliest forms of the looping technique.

Mending a fishing net using the same looping techniques and tools that fishermen have used for centuries. Split, Yugoslavia.

artifacts, one cannot help but wonder at their excellence of craftsmanship and speculate about the people who fashioned them. They were, in fact, leading the way to one of the world's most artistic achievements — the making of exquisite laces that centuries later would be the objects of national controversies that surrounded the Great Renaissance of Europe.

Techniques for creating lace have varied over the centuries according to the skills of its makers. Generally, many of the same methods that are found in the making of netting, tatting, looping, knitting, braiding, weaving macrame, and other forms of the art are evident. A knowledge of these techniques can lead a skilled observer to identify the source and perhaps even the maker of fine laces in much the same way a connoisseur of fine wines can identify the country and even the vineyard from which a rare and distinctive vintage has been created.

Trade routes, or those routes used for invasion, are known as the pathways along which the handicraft arts were to find their way between countries and across continents. Soldiers and merchants bundled their clothing to take along with them and pieces especially prized were no doubt shown to the envy of others around distant campfires.

Since the very earliest prehistoric times, important commercial centers developed along these trade and invasion routes. They were major hubs of activity and most made their unique imprint upon the textile arts.

As early as 2000 B.C., sailors plying these waters are known to have transported their netting techniques along the pointing arm of the Mediterranean. From very early times, the Phoenicians are one such culture famous in history for their exploits in commerce and navigation. They could weave exotic woolen and linen cloth and often dyed and sewed the cloth into actual garments for trading. Establishing colonies in Spain, Italy, and Northern Africa, they influenced much of the developing Western culture even before the ancient Greeks. They dominated the region and were fairly called the culture from the "Middle of the Earth" because their territory connected Europe with Asia and Africa.

Many other ancient civilizations thrived and developed over a very long period of time — from thousands of years before Christ to about 500 A.D. These ancient civilizations, such as the Persians, Egyptians, Assyrians, and Babylonians, were followed by the classic cultures of the Greeks, Romans, and the Byzantines. History records an abiding and continual interest from these ancient cultures in the textile arts. The development and flow of the needle arts were nourished and spread. Techniques for the making and dyeing of fine cloths were refined — the arts pressing forward to ever-higher levels of achievement in the presence or shadow of constant brutal war and conflict.

Assyrian Cuneiform tablets from the 8th Century B.C., as seen in the British National Museum. They offer clues to the ancient lifestyles and include information about ancient textiles .

A library of ancient Assyrian clay tablets was discovered at Nineveh that was painstakingly written and assembled by King Ashurbanipal. He was known as the "King of the World, King of all the Four Rims of the Earth, King of Kings, and Prince Without Rival." In the nearly 300 tablets found, a history of the entire lifestyle and culture can be reconstructed through translation of their ancient cuneiform language and blocked symbols.

The making of fine garments and the embellishments of style that was added to them was obviously of great importance to the Ancient

Relief panel of an Assyrian King from the 8th Century B.C. On display at the British National Museum.

Assyrians. There are repeated references to the arts of making fabrics and stitching assembled pieces together for clothing. King Ashurbanipal himself is described as "lavishly attired in robes of the finest woven and trimmed arrayment." But, the magnificence of the ancient kingdom of Babylonia — the "Gate of God" — offers modern researchers one of the most complete panoramas of culture and lifestyle known to the civilized world between 2700 and 500 B.C. The "Hanging Gardens," considered one of the Seven Wonders of the World, the vaulted temples, intricate language, engraved jewelry, art objects in gold, silver, ivory, and the elaborate works in fine woven, pulled, and drawn cloth, established that Babylonia was no stranger to the mystery of beautiful design.

Rulers such as Nebuchadnezzar, Cyrus the Great, and Alexander the Great were not only brilliant in battle, but devoutly encouraging to innovations in artistic achievement — particularly with regard to their costly personal clothing and gemstone adornments that "captured the lights and eternal radiance of the gods they believed they were."

Translations of primitive Chaldaic, Arabic, and Hebrew manuscripts, pictographs and drawings from earlier cave dwellers, and the etched walls of tombs in ancient Egypt, reveal that the creative spirit — often called the essence of mankind — has survived throughout the ages. The need to create is central to the human soul. The skills necessary to develop useful tools, to beautify what we wear, and to provide the satisfaction that comes only through doing, are enduring values that transcend both time and place.

In early times however, netting, weaving, and other forms of what we now call "lace" had strictly utilitarian purposes. Survival. Many hundreds of years were to pass before the ancients began to realize that if they used less dense, more delicate fibers, they could embellish and enhance more completely the clothing they wore — that by weaving closely knotted materials together, they could fashion, fringe, and make their clothing more attractive — perhaps be more enviable to others in the primitive villages. And, where they once decorated their favorite fishing nets with beautiful shells found along the shore, or with stones washed smooth by the tides and sand, they discovered ways to fasten these and other ornaments to themselves and to their clothing.

From the records of ancient times, we also know that no distinction was made between what we now know as "networks," "netting," "weaving," "embroidery," or "lace." The terms were used interchangeably. The Prophet Isaiah, for example, in Chapter 19, Verse 9 of the Bible, spoke of ancient artists who "work in fine flax, weaving networks." At that time, royal figures wore robes of colored silks embroidered with strands of gold, silver, and precious gems.

Plain, twill, and satin weaves — the three main kinds of weaving — were well-known throughout the civilized world by at least 1000 B.C. Threads strung upon frames formed a background through which a wood, bone, or ivory shuttle was passed as a crosswise weft or woof. Woven fabrics were produced to reflect the culture, time, and place, but the basic looming technique characterizes the art — world wide.

Fringes, common to all hand-woven fabrics, are a result of "leftover" lengthwise threads attached to the tops and bottoms of looms. Tied to keep the material from unraveling after being removed from the looms, these fringes were often separately knotted, embroidered, or tasseled to make decorative borders — the basis for the later, more sophisticated embellishment of the lace arts.

In the book of Exodus, there are several references to the fact that embroidery was common at the time of Moses. Ezekiel describes both

Egyptian and Syrian embroideries, and examples of early netting and darning can be found in many of the old Babylonian sculptures. Even then, ornamentation was described in terms of the human motivations that have always been involved in the wearing of adornment. In Isaiah Chapter 3, Verse 23, we are cautioned not to "value fine ornamentation above more godly pursuits."

18th Century Greek head covering edged with fringe. National Historic Museum, Greece.

Later, as we shall see, many government sanctions and policies against the use of lace were issued "lest the wearer cease to be godly and humble in his own eyes and become an abomination in the eyes of the one and true God."

Mummy wrappings found in Egyptian and Graeco-Roman tombs are lavishly embroidered and can be identified with the more sophisticated kinds of open designs that we now refer to simply as "lace." They seemed to have worked their lace-like designs by drawing threads out of the body of a fabric itself and then tied their designs together into decorative patterns.

Excavations also resulted in the finding of bone tools and other implements that have long been asso-

ciated with the decorative arts of lace-making. From excavations at Mycenae, on the Greek mainland which dates from 1600 to 1100 B.C., garments woven of gold, silver, jewels, copper and other precious metals have been found. Embellished armaments, and elaborate drawings of richly-decorated clothing have been discovered that show the arts of braiding, weaving, and stitching fashioned by highly skilled hands.

Along the Aegean Sea, between 3000 and 1100 B.C., some of the main centers of civilization were the Minoan, Helladic, Cycladic, and Troadic cultures, known for their architectural masterpieces and flourishing textile industries.

In Homer's writings dating back to the 850s B.C., there are numerous references to "nets woven of gold." His descriptions in the "Iliad" of "finely woven hangings" closely resemble what we now call "darned networks" used for curtain edgings and articles of clothing.

Pictures and descriptions from the far-flung Roman Empire — steadily developing to the stature of a world civilization for over 1000 years — between 753 B.C. when Rome was founded to its fall in 476 A.D., when Romulus Augustus was its last emperor — provide historical perspective on the uses of adornment and the values placed upon it for personal ornamentation. A type of Roman toga, for example, called "scultulata vestis," used an open mesh or net to create fabulous designs. Designs were held together into patterns that were "costly beyond measure and

Network on an Ancient Egyptian Mummy. Courtesy of the British National Museum.

were more valued than gemstones to those who could purchase them or have patience to wait for their completions when commissioned."

Later, and through the Middle Ages, the Turks, also called the Moors, conquered nations and carried their culture along with them. They were establishing an even greater taste for fine embroideries and fine, delicate personal adornment throughout a vast area that ranged from the mountains of Tibet in the East and that huge territory through the Mediterranean, Italy, Spain, Austria, Greece, and other European countries such as Yugoslavia. Their skilled artisans made articles with threads of silk, gold, and silver — to adorn their dresses, to ornament the veils which their cultures required be worn on their heads, and to display their individual creative skills.

Examples of this antiquity are evident in the "oyas" of Turkey which can be traced back through time to 2000 B.C. These skills, techniques, and designs that originated in the Anatolia region of Turkey are known for their exotic Arabesque patterns and delicate flowers which have become a national pride in craftsmanship, known even today as "the art that speaks."

"Oya" means beautiful in the Turkish language and this artform represents a legacy of tradition with a style unique to Turkey. This technique embraces the culture, the love, the hope, and the pain, and the delights of humor. Through a specific arrangement of colors, motifs, and floral design, this needlework can express the feelings of the wearer and communicate those feelings without words — without reprisal.

For example, using green color in the oya worn by a new bride announces happiness, but wearing red pepper motifs means that the new bride is not getting along well with her husband. Yellow symbolizes fatigue, the rose symbolizes beauty and youth, white hyacinths promise fidelity, and a girl in love wears purple hyacinths.

The Arabic influence gave direction to the handicraft arts and each art became more uniquely different in each culture. Even the terms used in Western Europe to describe the lace arts have their roots in the Arabic world. The Italian word "ricano" means embroidery and comes from the old Arabic work "Rabuna;" the Italian word "trine" means lace and comes from the old Arabic word "Targe."

During the Middle Ages, in their effort to reclaim the Holy Land, the Crusaders also did their part to transport the traditions and tastes of the Western Empire to other parts of the world as well as to return with items and ideas from the East.

In fact, some garments owned by the Vatican in Rome date back to 1298 A.D. and represent many exquisite examples of cut work, drawnwork, and embroidered vestments. An alb, worn by Pope Boniface VIII at the turn of the 13th Century, probably made its way into Rome by way of the Turkish invasion during the 10th Century.

After the European countries were able to overthrow the Turkish occupation of their lands, they developed into conquering, colonizing powers in their own right. They each took their place in history by introducing new ideas in design and adaptation of the needlecrafts to tell their own story and to express their spirit of creativity and national pride. As centuries passed, the trade routes continued to be channels of distribution for the developing arts. The arts unique to each country have long been an important means of communication between peoples of all lands. They provide a backdrop against which lifestyles, hardships, victories, rivalries, wars, and peace can be appreciated.

For example, Spain ruled the seas with its invincible galleons and the scores of armies that touched the lives of millions in every distant corner of the world. They used the design patterns established by ancient cultures of the past in architecture and textiles and adapted them to express the Spanish culture.

Southern Spain, a Moorish stronghold for over 800 years, has long been a region of cultural diversity with an international flavor. Mixtures of

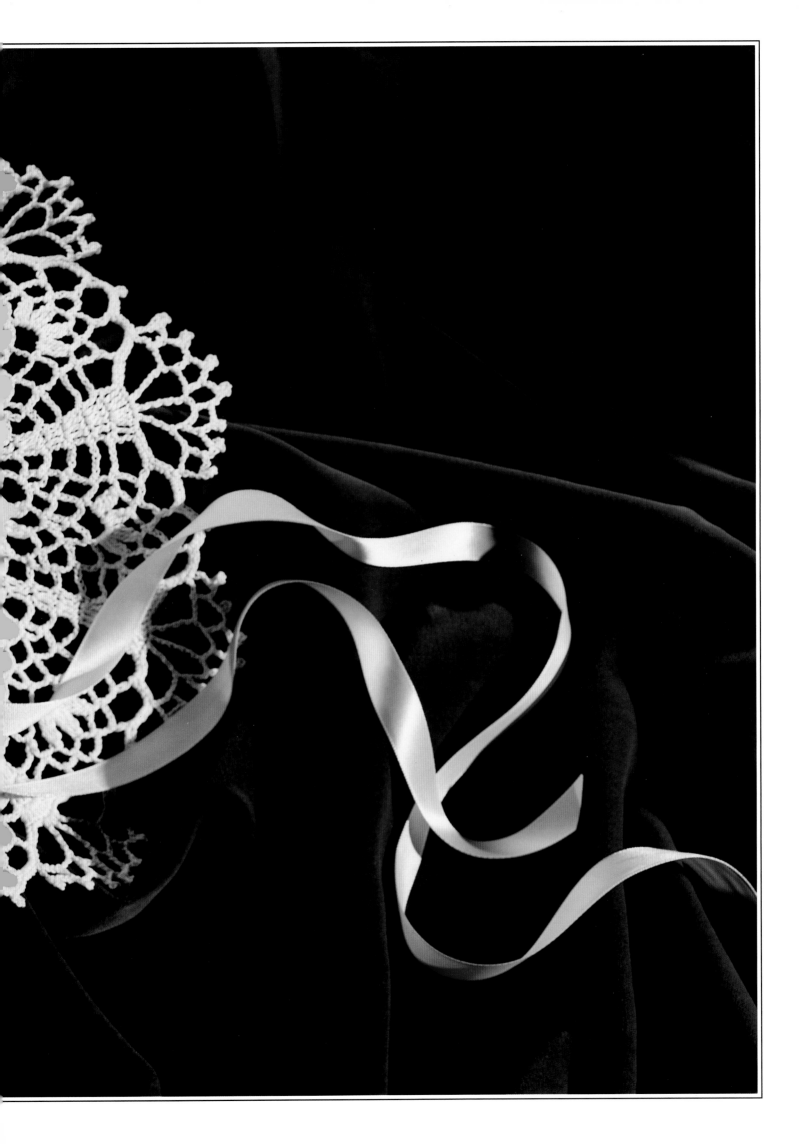

tradition are evident in everything from architecture to patterns in lace — from the spires of churches to the tiles found in sidewalks and streets.

Historians generally agree that the needle we recognize today — a sliver of metal with an eyelet at one end and a sharp point at the other — was a product of Asiatic Turkey. During the Middle Ages, needles were carried by the Arab traders into Spain and other parts of the Mediterranean region. Coming then to be known as the "Spanish Needle," this simple yet revolutionary device was later produced in greater quantities during the reign of Queen Elizabeth in 1565. Usefulness of this Arab invention was apparent, and by the start of the Industrial Revolution, English manufacturers were turning out needles by the thousands.

The shortest trade routes between the Near East and the trade ports of Italy, Spain, France, England, and Ireland, pass through the country of Yugoslavia. Settled with villages dotting its ragged coastline on the Adriatic, it has long been established as an important geographical hub. Protected coves and more than 1200 islands have offered sanctuary for travelers since earliest recorded history. As a regular stopping place for some, and a permanent home for others, its territorial waters became well-known to all travelers.

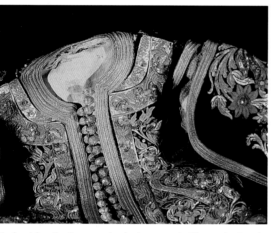

Embroidered velvet warrior jacket worn in Greece during the time of the Turkish occupation. It represents a continuation of the traditional Byzantine Art of embroidery from the fall of Constantinople in 1453 up through the 20th Century. Courtesy of Natural Historic Museum of Greece.

Settled since Neolithic times, Yugoslavia is centered in this region so important to the history of lace-making. Here, there is a richness of tradition and an artistic dominance that began with the founding of their largest Illyrian colonies. Built before and during the expansion years of the Ancient Roman Empire, these communities along the Adriatic provide a study in contrasts. Its history is a rich mixture of cultures and folklore. Yugoslavia represents a mixture of the oldest cultures on the European Continent. Even today, some of the people practice many ancient traditions much as they were performed hundreds of years ago.

Lace and lace-making is the story of people — kings and queens — of hopes and ambitions of commoners. It is a story of aspiration, of dreams, and of dedication. Lace — exquisite personal adornment. Ornamentation. Perfection in style. It represents an eye-catching centerpiece for individuality and the expression of human skill and creativity; the work of caring and loving hands throughout centuries. Lace was the statement of high fashion for some, and the trade or craft that meant economic survival for others.

Lace — far more than a design in fabric, a falling collar about the neck, a ruffle on the sleeve, or a fringe on a handkerchief — has held its place of honor among people the world over as a personal, highly individual, and yet universal symbol of status.

To fully appreciate the modern art of crochet, or indeed any of the handicrafts as practiced by both men and women the world over, one must look back in time to catch some of the flavors and richness of lace-making — and to know something of the human spirit that led to its development as a separate and unique art form.

Embroidery, the art of embellishing a flat piece of cloth with colored silks, gold, or silver thread, has been considered a primary step in the advancement of lace. The Phrygians, from 1200 B.C., were the most noted for their exquisite embroideries of gold. The art flourished first among the ancient civilizations of the East, such as the Saracenic Linen from the 10th Century B.C. It continued to spread westward, and became so important through the ages that a great deal of time and money was dedicated to bringing it to perfection.

It continued to grow in importance and sophistication on a worldwide basis. For example, the Popes of Rome were collecting fine specimens from all over the world during the 16th Century.

Many of the embroideries are so magnificent in concept and coloring, that the finer pieces often resemble fine paintings. In fact, embroidery existed before painting and was probably the first medium that could depict objects of nature in their natural colors.

Pulled or Drawn Work is another important foundation in the sequence of lace development, and is known as one of the earliest types of open work embroidery. It involved the drawing out or pulling together of the threads in a plain weave fabric, creating the holes necessary for the creation of an openwork design. Drawn work was used most often to ornament shrouds, altar cloths and other ecclesiastical items.

Drawn work was popular all over Europe and was called Punto Tirato in Italy during the Middle Ages. In fact, it was a favorite lace technique of the powerful Italian Medici house. Many of the aprons and collars of that period were trimmed with very fine drawn work.

However, specimens of this technique have been discovered as far back in history as ancient Egypt. Those pieces were worked on fine linen and later the remaining threads outside of the design were buttonholed together to form a ground.

Cut Work is an English name given to another very early lace form. It had been known in Italy as Punto Tagliato since the 12th Century where it was practiced within the cloistered walls of the convents to decorate the priest's robes and grave cloths.

During the 14th Century, it was used to decorate household linens as well as church items. By the 15th to the 17th Century, it was an art practiced by aristocratic ladies who made expensive gifts for the church and others as well as ornamenting their own fine goods with the technique. The first pattern books to mention cut work were published in 1543 by a Venetian called Pagano.

In cut work, design was embroidered and then parts of the fabric cut away leaving open spaces for thread designs to be worked in. In

Early 18th Century sample of drawn work originally from the Aegean Islands. The designs in the lace work are of symbolic importance. Displayed in the National Historic Museum, Greece.

Drawn work sample from the late 19th Century worked with thin embroidery thread. Typically used in Greek homes. Displayed in the National Historic Museum, Greece.

drawn work, which was the basis of Reticella, the designs were very geometric. Cut work allowed a more free flowing design with curved lines. The development of these two early forms of lace eventually led to the first needlepoint laces called "punto in aria," meaning "stitches in the air," in which the foundation fabric was done away with. It was a lace quilt literally made in the air.

Needlepoint laces are worked entirely by hand with a needle against a design drawn on parchment or other backing material. Most often using two thicknesses of linen stitched together, a skeletal pattern is then formed by stitching down linen thread over the outlines of the pattern drawn on the parchment. Then, the meshes and solid parts of the design are filled in. The various parts are joined by ties or bars. These bars are decorated with smaller knots or picots, which is a characteristic of Venetian Rose Point Lace. Other technique variations may be seen in other laces, such as Point d'Alencon or Point d'Argentan.

Once a pattern or design is completed, the lace is separated from the backing by carefully passing a knife between the two layers of linen and cutting all of the connecting threads. The lace is lifted from the backing and you have "stitches in

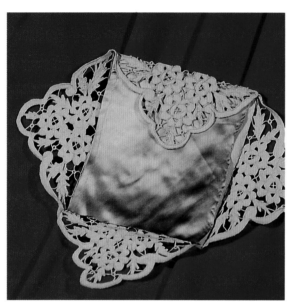

Late 19th Century breadholder created with cut work and satin. On display in the National Historic Museum, Greece.

Late 19th Century cut work, referred to as Athenian embroidery. On display in the National Historic Museum, Greece.

the air" with no background fabric to hold them together.

Punto in aria was an innovative, free flowing technique that opened the way for astonishing new design possibilities and led directly to the world renowned "Venetian Rose Point" — considered by royalty the world over to be the treasure of kings and queens — the stuff of dreams — the symbol of wealth and status.

True lace which evolved from drawn work and cut work is defined as "an ornamental openwork formed of threads made with flax, cotton, silk, gold, silver, mohair, or aloe fiber that is plaited, looped or twisted together." The word "lace" is derived from the Latin word "laqueus" (noose), and from the French "lassis," or "lacis," which means "knotted network."

Brought to a peak of its perfection in the 16th, 17th, and 18th Centuries, principally in Italy, Spain, Belgium, and France, the owning and wearing of lace reached a level of intensity that was often an obsession. More valued than the riches of a king's treasury, lace became a symbol of wealth, power, and strength for nations.

Historically, technically, and artistically, the aficionado of handmade lace is most interested in two types of production: needle laces and bobbin laces. Both of these broad categories of lace-making gradually evolved through the Middle East to Western Europe and led the lace arts to a new level of sophistication and meaning. Accepted literature of lace history shows that a number of countries were producing laces of varying designs and quality as early as the 14th and 15th Centuries, such as Flanders, Italy, Sweden, Russia, Spain, Germany, and England.

From the 14th Century through the 17th Century, in Italy, Flanders, Scandinavia, and indeed throughout Western Europe, the art of lace-making was steadily refined. To the very best artisans, lace-making became a respected trade, along with jewelry-making, silversmithing, and other specialized crafts that required a high degree of proficiency, dedication to the art, and extreme patience. Designers worked with the drawn thread patterns and evolved some breathtakingly lavish individual pieces of lace as testimony to their developed skills.

Many of their designs, especially in the early stages of the art's development, were geometric in both structure and form — a direct descendant of the styles used during earlier times for the making of primitive fishing nets. Many interesting pieces of the traditional geometric works used darned and decorated patterns that included glass beads, precious gems, or other passimenterie — no doubt an inspiration of technique passed down from mother to daughter, from father to son. Many examples can be found today of early Italian lace arts often called "reticello" — a name that has now become associated with all laces having geometric patterns.

Italy, often given credit for the invention of lace, commanded a major share of the world's markets for many generations of a growing industry. Italian laces offer a special and innovative beauty. The country's styles and uses of laces are distinctive. Pervasive.

In Italy, virtuosos of the craft took the art of lace-making to its finest levels of development. Multiples of designs, stunning new effects, variations on techniques, combining the best ideas into textured or "engraved" patterns, are all Italian lace hallmarks of achievement and considered by their owners to be more valuable than gold.

Bobbin lace or bone lace, often inaccurately called pillow lace, were also developed from ancient techniques. It was first called bone lace because the bones from fish or animals were used instead of pins and bobbins. In fact, in the very early days, some lace makers used the fingers of a few to several men as pegs for the twisting of their threads.

With the inventions of bobbins, pins, and pillows, exquisite interwoven designs were created when each strand of thread was tied to the narrow neck of a single bobbin and worked separately.

Hundreds of bobbins hung over a pillow and were manipulated by hand. The individual threads were crossed, twisted, and plaited to produce the lace as required by a pattern that had been drawn on paper or parchment in advance. Work done with bobbins has a resemblance to weaving and can look very much like muslin or have the appearance of needlepoint lace that uses closely-tied rows of button-hole stitches.

There are also clues that help to establish the beginning of this art and its growing sophistication simultaneously with the development of the needle-laces. A tombstone in

Punto in Aria, 17th Century. Courtesy of the Victoria and Albert Museum.

Annaberg, Germany, for example, announces: "Here lies Barbara Uttmann, died 14th January, 1575, whose invention of lace in the year 1561 made her the benefactress of the Hartz Mountains."

While some controversy surrounds Ms. Uttmann's "invention," there is little doubt that she was the first to introduce bobbin lace into Germany. She worked with the mountain girls in her mining community and later set up work shops and created new, simple patterns.

From family inventory records, portraits painted during the Middle Ages in Western Europe, and from wardrobe accounts found of violators of the many "Sumptuary Laws," designed to regulate and control the wearing of lace as excessively "consumptive," it is clear that by any defi-

Reticella, 17th Century. Courtesy of the Victoria and Albert Museum.

nition, lace was produced in Italy and in a number of other countries prior to the year 1500. Religious leaders, noble families, and officials of state used lace as a symbol of privileged rank, status, power and wealth.

Dante, writing in the "Divina Commedia," a work begun in the year 1307 and considered a masterpiece of world literature, as well as in his Italian collection of love poems called "La Vita Nuova," points to the uses of lace as "giving way to extravagance and luxury with many rich people impoverishing themselves by excessively purchasing scarves, sashes, mantles, coverlets, cushions of gold brocade embroidered with pearls and other gems, and veils and trimmings of lace made with spun gold, of immoderate richness."

As early as the 14th Century, Greek Guilds were developing rapidly. They brought new ideas to old customs and were primarily responsible for establishing powerful new commercial ventures in the handicraft arts that were to have a profound influence on the whole of Europe. After the Turkish occupation in 1453, whole families of Greeks were migrating to Western Europe for religious and political reasons. They settled in the same cities where the early Greek traders had settled. By the 15th Century, there was a significant number of Greek immigrants living in Venice. In fact, the Greek language and Hellenic customs were common throughout the area.

The Greek women brought their lace with them and continued to wear it and use it to decorate their homes. These women continued to develop the art, and it was also learned by many aristocratic Roman families.

The records of the powerful Milanese Sforza family, in part belonging to the Hellenized noble family of Naxos, indicate that the antique Greek Lace called Radexello was brought to Milan before 1493.

The personal family records of Angela and Heppolita Sforza, Viconti of Milan, provide a complete inventory of family wealth that was divided between their daughters upon the death of the Elder Sforza. The castle, situated in the Province of Venice, properties surrounding it, and virtually every item of possessions are listed in the family documents dated September 12, 1493. Included in the nearly 200 pages of family inventories, are lists of "Ricamo a Reticella," "Lavoro a Groppi," "Lavoro ad ossa," and "Punti dei Dodisi Fusi."

All of these works represent the early documentation of the existence of the fine embroideries, networks, and laces known to have developed in the late 15th to early 16th Centuries. Many are represented in design books of the period. In fact, "Punto in Aria" first appeared in a pattern book by Passarotti printed in Bologna 1591

Venetian Rose Point, 17th Century. Courtesy of the Victoria and Albert Museum.

and was a lace to be made completely apart from the main fabric.

It is interesting that the lace art reached the peak of perfection in the same countries where painting also reached a peak of perfection, and that the laces of the periods were depicted in detailed portraits painted at the time. From the 16th Century, the development of lace, its variations in design and fashion became easier to study because of this representation in commissioned oil paintings. Sumptuary laws, developing pattern books and documents from convents and lace schools also gave new insights and documentation for the development of the lace arts.

Beatrice D'este Sforza, by Leonardo da Vinci. One of the earliest records of lace appeared in the inventory of the Sforza family in Italy in 1493. Courtesy of the Uffizi Gallery.

Policies or edicts referring to the lace industry were called "Sumptuary Laws." They were an important element in the development of lace because they were ever-present throughout the many stages of lace history. Italy, France, England, and many other countries of Western Europe imposed enormous taxes on the transportation of lace. They also established various restrictions on its uses by means of the Sumptuary Laws because lace was considered a national treasure that was suitable only for royalty in many of these countries.

The laws were designed to reduce or restrict the flow of lace in order to protect the value that each country placed upon their own lace industry. Countries were fiercely competitive with each other, and the production of fine laces provided great prestige and power to the aristocracy.

France passed the first sumptuary law in 608 A.D., in order to control the use of "high priced cloth" used for dress during that era. Penned by Charles the Great, the law was to encourage simplicity of dress for all the people and to restrain extravagance and luxury. Similar sumptuary laws were also enacted by other monarchs such as Phillip Augustus, Louis VIII, King Charles II, and Henri III.

Such laws varied of course, depending upon the personal convictions of each ruler as to what constituted "ostentatious adornment." For example, Louis XI refused to allow "those without titles to have the luxury of adorning their tables or their persons with gold, silks, or silver cloths." His permission was required for the making of any such extravagances except for uses by the Church.

King Charles II and Henri III absolutely forbade the ownership of "any articles of luxury except for himself, members of his own family, or his courtiers."

Obviously, this tendency toward simplicity for the masses hampered the development of fine laces. Even Venice, the leader in the development of lace, was hampered by these laws.

In 1299, the Great Council of Venice passed a sumptuary law which limited the wearing of any trimming that cost "more than five lire an ell." A few years later the Council's edicts on consumption included limits on the wearing of "any gold, silver, pearls, or precious gems." No child could be attired with precious materials or gold or silver adornments. However, above the age of twelve, girdles costing less than 25 ducats could be worn.

The laws and customs of 14th Century Europe also had their effect on the use of tools directly related to the lace industry. For example, pins in England were so scarce during that time that the Queen levied a tax to drive up the price of pins so that she would have plenty for herself.

Commoners could only buy pins on January One or January Two, and they saved all year in anticipation of their pin buying spree; so began the custom of always having "pin money." In France, pins were so popular that a princess ordered 12,000 at one time. These restrictions all served the purpose of keeping the commoner separated from the aristocracy.

Then, in the early 1400s, the women appealed directly to the Pope for relief from these strict edicts concerning dress. No doubt under

Queen Elizabeth I, 1588, wearing the exquisite needle-lace of the period. Courtesy of the National Portrait Gallery, London.

Catherine de Medici, became a legendary figure in the development of the Lace Industry in France during the 16th Century. Courtesy of the Scala Art Resource.

Mary, Queen of Scots, devoted to learning the various skills of needlework, created many beautiful articles with lace and embroidery. Courtesy of the National Portrait Gallery, London.

considerable pressure against such formidable odds, and upon hearing the long and impassioned arguments presented, he finally relented and gave his permission "for the wearing of the gauds."

Of particular interest is an edict passed into law in 1476 that specifically stated, "It is forbidden to use silver and embroidery on any fabric and to have in personal possession any Punto in Aria of linen threads made with a needle, or gold and silver threads."

In argument for yet another Edict from the Council of Venice, issued in 1504, it was stated for the record that "....among so many expenses, superfluous and useless, the women in this city show a vainglorious pomp which is most ruinous for the nobles and burgesses; that of changing so often the shape of dresses through the applications and embellishments of lacis ... a practice requiring the most severe controls if it is to be stopped." It would appear that the Council was steadily losing control in its battle to legislate humility.

Later, when lace-making continued to develop toward becoming the predominant industry of the 16th and 17th Centuries, Venice continued to create very stringent laws on the uses and transportation of its prestigious laces. Even death was set as the punishment for any extreme violation such as smuggling or teaching the lace arts in a foreign country.

Louis XIV of France alone issued more than twenty separate proclamations and "hundreds of official edicts" against the wearing of lace by anyone other than his Royal Family and chosen members of his court, even though he was subsidizing the lace industry. This was happening during the 17th Century, a time when the making and wearing of lace was at its peak in terms of Western European fashion. The competition in lace manufacture among France and Italy and other European countries was also at a peak. Fine lace was a necessary item in every aristocratic wardrobe in the world.

The sumptuary laws were only one of the many influences continually affecting the evolving lace arts. During the 16th and 17th Centuries, great events were sweeping through Western Europe that altered the course of history in every country. It was a period of growth and unprecedented development that touched every life, every mind, every soul.

The 16th Century. These were the days of Shakespeare. Sir Walter Raleigh. Spain no longer ruled the seas. The power of the sword gave way to a freedom of mind. Names like Spencer, Machiavelli, and Martin Luther became household words. It was a time for brilliant essays, as opposed to convincing victories on the battlefield. Education and a nurturing of the human spirit was common, as opposed to titles, rank, and position as a result of birth, that were common during the Middle Ages. This was a time of discovery, freedom, experimentation, and invention.

This age featured the "Renaissance Man." Leonardo da Vinci and others from the early Florentine school of painters were among the first to paint finely detailed portraits including lace. The Flemish painters also produced some of the world's best known costume pictures. The Spanish master, Velasquez, is also one of the most famous artists who painted in great detail the style of lace that was worn during the period. There are many fine portraits of aristocratic families, kings, queens, courtiers, and other nobles who wanted to assure

Elizabeth of Bohemia, 16th Century. Courtesy of the National Portrait Gallery, London.

dustry in the countries of Western Europe emerged. Fashion and prestige associated with fine lace became largely responsible for breathing new life into an ancient craft. Now, in the 16th Century, handmade lace, in the true modern sense of the word, was distinctly set apart from its earlier origins. Italy, particularly the Northern sections; Flanders, an area now known as Western Belgium, and Northern France were in the forefront of this exploding industry.

Italy claims to have been the first to develop and refine both the bobbin and needlelaces. Old traditions and the surge of new ideas combined to provide motivation and interest in the arts, sciences, and lace. Spain, Germany, Sweden, Russia, England, and others also contributed to the booming lace industry of the period.

During the reign of Queen Elizabeth I, needles were mass manufactured to exacting specifications. Cromwell soon formed a manufacturing company around the old "Spanish" needle at Redditch, Worcestershire, to make needles through a process that he invented. It is a process that was practiced in England for generations and one that established English needles as the finest in the world.

Almost simultaneously, these countries began producing

themselves a form of immortality throughout the known world.

Dressed in their finery, the subjects in these paintings are a rich source of historical knowledge about the laces of the period and reveal the high value given to the owning and wearing of lace.

During the 16th Century, the King of Denmark, Cavaliera Fiammingo, Mary Queen of Scots, Queen Elizabeth I, Charles of Savoy, Catherine deMedici, and hundreds of other noteworthy personages of the period were proudly shown in their portraits wearing high collars, rich brocades, edged ruffs about the neck, exotic braids, purlings, and narrow edgings of twisted threads. Most often, they were fashionably trimmed, edged, decorated and adorned with lace.

Separated not only by distance but by culture, a unique, thriving and profitable lace in-

Punto in Aria, late 16th Century Needlelace. Close-up of a similar Reticella worn by Elizabeth of Bohemia. Courtesy of the Victoria and Albert Museum.

Sir Thomas More, His Father, Household, and Descendants in the 16th Century wearing ruffs typical of the period. Courtesy of the National Portrait Gallery, London.

new lace patterns and styles — some gaining greater reputation for artistic value than others. Exquisite lace-making and respected lace makers were being scattered throughout Europe. Many of the best-known designers and artists received commissions to move to other countries and to meld their experience and skills with those found in their new land.

In style, laces produced were increasingly lavish, particularly so with the arrival of the new fashion — that of wearing decorative ruffs about the neck. Henry II of France is often credited with the invention because he first used it to hide a scar on his neck.

Another legendary figure of the 16th Century was Catherine de Medici. She was of a great and noble Italian family and became one of the foremost benefactors and devotees of fine lace. Catherine was ahead of her time and had an uncanny intuition for trend. After marrying King Henry II, she took her Italian laces to France and inspired her new country's lace-making industry with the help of the Venetian designer, Federico di Vinciolo.

Her tastes and interests in lace set her adopted country's style and leadership in the art.

France later became known throughout the civilized world because she had already encouraged and prized only the most exquisite demonstration of lace-making skill. This was the birth of an industry in France which was to become one of the most productive and influential centers of the art in Europe. She was active in many facets of needlework from fashion to teaching. In fact, it was Catherine who taught the young Mary, Queen of Scots to do needlework during her days in the French Court. Mary learned to create articles trimmed with lace and embroidery. She developed skills which later helped her to occupy the long hours of her imprisonment when her country was torn apart by the revolution.

Catherine believed that enormous expenditures for a wardrobe and other expensive items could turn the mind of man away from politics, war and other cares of the day.

She was also instrumental in the development of the French cosmetic industry and encouraged the use of ice cream, snuff, and libraries.

By the mid-16th Century, lace had come to mean much more than the stringed threads, cords, or ties of earlier days. It was more than drawing opposite edges together by arranging them in and out through eyelets or holes and pulling them tight — a process much like "lacing" boots, shoes, a blouse, or a decorative gown.

Now, it meant a fine ornamental design often embellished with or worked entirely with threads of gold and silver, and intricately drawn into distinctive designs, trimmings, and patterns. Lace was the contrast in or between fabrics — created by making

The Somerset House Conference in 1604, wearing ruffs typical of the period. Courtesy of the National Portrait Gallery, London.

strategically placed holes in it through which threads are passed to bind a design together — open and closed spaces — drawn tightly at some moments, left loose and filmy at others. The points of Venice were copied throughout the Continent and are perhaps best characterized in this period by the costly, impressive attire of Catherine de Medici. Venetian Point became the climax of needle lace and evolved into other variations, often being classed as Raised Point, Gros Rose, Flat Point, and eventually, the Raised Point de Venise.

The Venetian laces were clearly the most sought-after laces in the world. The style was distinctive, elaborate, and had emerged from the geometric Reticella and the Punto in Aria form that employed the simple buttonhole stitches. Contained in the ornate Venetian laces were decorative fillings, ornamental bars, and beautiful arrangements using padded outlines.

Venetian point laces often had densities of over 6,000 buttonhole stitches for every square inch of lace produced. They were at least ten times more dense and fine than any other kind of lace that would be produced for the next 300 years. Fine linen threads were used along with either sharply pointed or rather blunted needles, depending upon the particular design being worked at the moment.

Often, rather large, bulbous cushions, made especially for the purpose, were placed either on a worker's lap or upon a low stool in front of each lace maker. With needles, bobbins, and only the finest of threads, stitches were individually made against the pillow as backing.

This was the famous Venetian lace, unique to the Republic of Venice. It became characterized for its uses of a layered, dimensional effect through designs that incorporated diamond-shaped panes, bold contours, chevrons, holes, stripes, and "point d' esprit" in strong relief. The work provided a sense of perspective, and in feel, it held rhythmic textures that caught light and shadow. It was without doubt the most beautiful lace ever fashioned from the hand of man or woman.

At first, any attempts to copy the Venetian laces were little more than crude imitations. Gradually, however, workers in other countries added innovations of their own and produced some of their own distinctive works that came to be known and respected throughout the civilized world.

Henry, Prince of Wales, 1610, wearing lace trimmed collar and cuffs. Courtesy of the National Portrait Gallery, London.

Like Catherine de Medici, Queen Elizabeth I of England had a well-known special love for lace during the 16th Century. Her passion to

Mary Throckmorton, Lady Scudamore, 1632, wearing exotic needlelace. Courtesy of the National Portrait Gallery, London.

able to produce vast quantities of "Point d'Espagne." During the 16th Century, it consisted of colored silks as well as a lace made entirely of precious metals for the adornment of royalty. Often coarse and a heavy burden to wear, their laces were nevertheless perhaps the most expensive of any known lace in the entire history of lace-making. Few of them survived, however, because they were later melted down and used for their value as currency.

From the 16th and through the 17th Centuries, lace threads, fabrics, and lace-making techniques were steadily refined. Then, there was a sense of urgency to produce ever-newer and more exquisite styles. It was a period of grand experimentation. Competition for making, owning, and wearing only the latest of lace fashions became more intense, perhaps, than at any other time in the history of lace-making. The distinctive Venetian laces and their counterparts in other countries were at full flowering — delicate, extravagant, glorious maturity as a unique art form. The many paintings of the era done by Goya, Van Dyke, and other masters help to recall the inspired beauty and magic that was embodied in the Renaissance Laces of Europe.

With the increasing popularity of Point de Venise, the famous ruff so characteristic of the 16th Century began to be replaced in the 17th Century by collars that were deeply scalloped and made entirely with lace, or at least richly trimmed in lace.

Laces were made to flow from the shoulders to fringes on sleeves and even from the tops of men's polished boots. Ladies caps, gloves, handkerchiefs, capes, garment hems, handbags, and of

acquire and wear only the most costly and elaborate gowns resulted in a wardrobe of more than 3,000 of them. Most of them were gracefully trimmed with lace embellishments and some — over 200 of them — had precious gemstones sewn into the fabric "in rippling patterns to catch the light of her every movement."

Laces made in England won universal admiration. Notable production centers operated at Devonshire, Buckinghamshire, Northhamptonshire, and Bedfordshire. All were producing laces worthy of meeting the extravaganences of royalty.

Spain, because it possessed the greatest national reserves of gold and silver at the time, was

Frances, Countess of Somerset, 1615, wearing needlepoint lace. Courtesy of the National Portrait Gallery, London.

beyond the top of the wearer's dramatic coiffure. Some must have thought of it as a bit garish, for by the year 1613 the Queen announced that the "wearing of such laces and embroideries are herewith forbidden."

In 17th Century England, preachers were extolling the virtues of humility in the eyes of God. They saw lace as an extravagance of sheer vanity and disclaimed its value as a whim of fancy and one that was not to be tolerated. Writer Ben Johnson commented, "Men think nothing of turning four or five hundred acres of their best lands into two or three trunks of apparel." The Church of England once

Endymion Porter, 1626, wearing a ruff. Courtesy of the National Portrait Gallery, London.

Bulstrode Whitelock, 1634, wearing a ruff. Courtesy of the National Portrait Gallery, London.

course the layers of silk undergarments popular in the day, were either entirely made of lace or expensively adorned with it in cascading flounces.

Children were also richly trimmed with all manner of laces on, under, and between layers of clothing. Lace surrounded their lives from the cradle with its inevitable canopy coverlet, to the lace fringed toys that they cherished.

Many royal families publicly denounced the use of lace and embroideries for commoners, while they demanded ever-increasing supplies and fresh designs for themselves. Many of the outrageous styles were made for the sole purpose of impressing others with the "power of the purse."

The "Medici Collar," so named for the style popularized by Marie de Medici in the 17th Century, was worn throughout Europe. It was a rigid upswept collar that was worn at the back of the shoulder line with some of them reaching

announced that "no man or woman wearing ruffs will be admitted to the Church." Lord Bacon himself said from his high office of State that "our English dames are much given to the wearing of costly laces, especially if brought from Italy, or France, or Flanders, as they are held in much esteem."

In spite of traditional attempts to restrain the uses of trimmings and gaudiments among the English people, the lace industry continued to flourish in the 17th Century. At the peak of its development, "Point 'd Angleterre" was created and produced along with other world-famous laces such as Honiton.

Laces were owned and worn by the upper classes throughout England across at least a century of time. Increasing amounts of lace in wider ranging styles and patterns were demanded as a matter of both taste and fashion, and naturally

Arthur, 1st Baron Capel and his family in 1604 wearing lace of the period. Courtesy of the National Portrait Gallery, London.

more workers were needed at that time to produce them.

Meanwhile in France, during the reign of Louis XIV, French lace took on a style and creativity of its own, and began to rival the renowned Italian laces. In French history, this was the period known as "Le Grande Monarque," a period when the French laces were world-class treasures in terms of dramatic style and perfection of workmanship. Louis XIV married the Spanish Infanta, and so the Spanish laces also became very popular and were often worn over gowns of exquisite silver and gold brocades.

Jean Baptiste Colbert was the powerful French Minister at the time. He became very concerned about the importation of Venetian laces and the amount of money flowing out of France as a result. Laws were passed to forbid the use of foreign lace. Colbert then bribed some of the best Italian lace designers and makers to come to France in order to teach and organize the budding French lace industry. A factory near Alencon was established, and the lace that was produced there soon rivaled and even surpassed the workmanship of many Italian laces.

Lace centers were established in more than a dozen cities. Laces created in these centers were to become known by the name of the center such as Rheims, Alencon, Sedan, Argentan, and others. Point 'd France, or Point 'd Colbert, became prized for their technique and creative substance. Colbert was determined that "Fashion should be to France what the mines of Peru were to Spain."

Lighter and finer laces were produced in the centers. France became a dominant force in the lace trade, and also set the latest fashion trends for lace throughout all the courts of Europe. These laces were innovations of the Venetian laces, but soon developed their own unique flavor and intricate beauty. Each commanded a place of high honor and esteem by the royalty of Western Europe. Each was considered the "most lavishly expensive with its embellishments and flowering suitable for the highest offices of kings, queens, and officials of state."

Clothing was not the only application for these beautiful, expensive laces. Laces were used to trim bed furniture, bath covers, linens, val-

Prince James Francis Edward Stuart and Louisa Maria Theresa, 1695. Courtesy of the National Portrait Gallery, London.

ances, church altars and many other articles. Royalty offered robes, collars, cravats, and other lace articles to the favored members of their court. The French lace industry, at its peak, was valued at millions of livres a year.

Then, still during the 17th Century reign of Louis XIV, disaster struck the French lace industry. The Edict of Nantes was revoked, and the best lace makers were soon scattered all over Western Europe. They immigrated to places where religious toleration existed. France lost thousands of its best lace workers to foreign countries within the space of a few years.

At the end of the 17th Century and during the 18th lace and lace-making continued to be an important, high-priced industry world wide. Every kind of lace for almost every kind of application became popular. Great fortunes were spent on acquiring the most ornate ruffles and jabots. During the 18th Century, the use of lace was less confined to nobility. English footmen and even servants were now wearing clothing trimmed with lace. Sometimes the laces were actually worked by the wearer for personal use, and not necessarily for sale.

Lace production was encouraged in a number of ways. In 1775, Queen Charlotte of England founded a lace-making school specifically "for employing the female infants of the poor in the blonde and black silk lace-making and thread laces." She recognized that once trained in this technique, even the youngest of children could accomplish the simple tasks of learning the basic stitches. By attending schools, they would have adequate care while being taught a useful skill that could lead to a lifetime profession.

An English poet of the period expressed the values of lace-making with these lines "... It will increase their peace, enlarge their store, to use their tongues less, and their needles more; The needle's sharpnesse profit yields pleasure, but sharpnesse of the tongue bites out of measure."

During this time in Italy, Pointe de Venise was still in demand, although the style had become lighter than the earlier version. Burano Point, the graceful and delicate needle lace, was also at a peak.

In 18th Century Spain, mantillas were in their finest form and were very popular among all the classes — from peasant to aristocrat. The flounces of lace added to the bottom of dresses was

Jean Baptiste Colbert, 1655. French Minister who was influential in the development of the French Lace Industry. Courtesy of the New York Metropolitan Museum.

so popular, the style developed into the national Spanish dress.

The very name, "lace," by the 18th Century was inexorably linked to images of personal status, power, authority, refinement, and class — it was socially desireable and increasingly attainable for everyone in Western Europe.

Around 1774 in France, during the reign of Louis XVI and his wife Marie Antoinette, the art of lace-making and lace wearing experienced its "finest hour." At the same time, revolutionary changes were in the wind. Among the strengthening of lower middle classes, there was a rising consciousness of the outrageous extravagance of the upper class. They were on the edge of revolt.

Marie Antoinette was often frivolous and seemingly unaware of this revolutionary spirit and unrest among the commoners. She loved fine lace as well as all the luxuries of the day. She wanted to be the best-dressed woman in France. Her passion for beauty clouded her vision in the midst of great danger. She was unhappy and constrained by her duties in the court and built an illusion of grand style around herself as a means of escape.

Public outcry against her and her husband's blatantly extravagant lifestyle amid the abject poverty of the people continued to grow. The masses rose up and demanded an end to their aristocracy. Louis XVI was executed. After four years in a cold, dark French prison, Marie longed for her death. On October 16, 1793 she asked for spiritual pardon for herself and for her enemies.

The executioner bound her hands and cut her famously beautiful hair. With her head bowed, she was led to her demise. Revolutionary women hurled obscenities at her. All of Paris witnessed her death. The spirit of opulence that surrounded her and her court was over.

The guillotine and the French Revolution of that period marked the end of the art of lace-making as it had been known in all of Western Europe. The aristocrats and nobility, the main users of lace, were either executed or had to flee and live as downtrodden refugees in foreign countries. Along with lace, women as a whole were dethroned. The age of privilege and extravagant beauty had come to an abrupt end.

The mood of the times demanded a return to a simpler style, more modest designs, and the end of extravagant embellishment. The public willed to "crush out every vestige of class distinctions that only enormous wealth could acquire."

The ghosts of the 18th Century continues to touch the lives and fashion of people. The trend of fashion changes to meet the flow of popular interest. However, the spirit of being fashionable, as characterized by the 18th Century has always been a need in the human soul. Fashion is a mirror that reflects the beliefs of the times.

Napoleon, seizing power in 1799 at the end of the French Revolution, wanted to revive and rebuild the dying lace manufacturing centers of France. He had a special love of fine ornamentation, and he also recognized that a revived lace industry could strengthen the post-revolution

Marie Antoinette with her children at Versailles. Her passion for beauty and extravagance helped create the "finest hour" for lace and lace-making in 18th Century France. Courtesy Giraudon Art Resource.

economy in France. He concentrated on the Alencon area and ordered a large amount of lace-trimmed bed furniture after his marriage to Marie Louise. He made the wearing of lace in his court mandatory, and so caused a renewed spark in the industry.

However, France never recovered its world-renowned position for the creation of fine lace which characterized the earlier days of "Le Grand Monarque." Many of the old lace-makers died and there were fewer and fewer young artists to take their place.

Thanks in part to the Napoleonic Era and its strict policies, France steadily rebuilt its undisputed position as the "fashion capitol of the world" — a recognition for excellence in design that the country has maintained ever since.

By the beginning of the 19th Century, handmade lace-making was a dying art throughout Western Europe. Many wealthy women attempted to revive the art, but the dawn of machine-made lace was making the handmade variety less popular and too expensive. After the invention of bobbin net in 1818, all lace later produced was considered "modern." Queen Adelaide ordered a complete dress of Honiton lace to be applied to machine-made net in order to benefit both the manual labor and the machine industry.

Then, there was somewhat of a revival in the art of handmade lace in Western Europe during the latter part of the 19th Century when lace was once again a popular item in a woman's wardrobe. Antique pieces were especially sought after. An outstanding example is Queen Victoria of England, who was especially fond of fine lace and wore much of it during her reign. During Victorian times, laces were used to trim tables, dressers, sheets, piano stools, flower pots, picture frames and everything else that touched the eye. Another example of this renewed period of interest in lace

Queen Adelaide, 1800s. Courtesy of the National Portrait Gallery, London.

is the Empress Eugenie of France. She once ordered a lace dress that took thirty-six lace workers about eighteen months to complete. It probably would have taken a single lace-maker at least 30 years to finish that dress.

From the 16th through the 19th Centuries, lace-making was an art that was known and practiced by creative individuals. Their pride of craftsmanship and dedication to their art, led to the unprecedented level of popularity and demand for their work. Many of the finest pieces of lace made during this period were produced for major exhibitions and fairs as a means of demonstrating expertise.

It was in the confines of the convents, lace schools and aristocratic circles themselves where the techniques of the art were to be nurtured and refined.

LACE: STARTS MODERN INDUSTRY
AND BECOMES A TRADITION

Wherever the work was done, it consumed many long hours of dedicated skill to complete just a single piece. Using the traditional patterns and designs of either the 16th or the 17th Century, for example, a pair of trimmed jacket cuffs made entirely of lace could consume up to nine months to make. That assumes a working schedule of eighteen hours a day, six days a week by a single skilled worker. Making a traditional dress front in needle lace would take most of a year to complete, if six workers were to spend nineteen to twenty hours a day, six days a week. Other examples of the time taken to produce single items of adornment show that even a pair of men's ruffles would take a single worker at least ten months to make if that worker labored at the task for at least fifteen hours a day, six days a week!

History also records that at least a dozen lace-makers were required to produce "a single ruff of modest proportions" during the 16th Century and beyond, especially when ruffs were at their peak of popularity in Spain, England, and France. Even with many hands working on a single piece, these ruffs of "modest proportions" might take a minimum of "at least a year or more" to produce.

Napoleon once made an order for a complete dress of lace that he intended to give as a rare and exquisite gift for his first wife. At one time, more than seventy workers were employed on the project and at no time were there fewer than thirty. Years passed and she died before it was ever completed. He gave it to his second wife instead.

Lace-edged handkerchiefs, by contrast, could be turned out in "less than a single month by one or two workers," particularly if held to the three or four inches in size that were in such great demand during the 1700s.

With increasingly popular and varied application for laces, however, more and more people became involved in its production over the centuries. At certain times in history, lace-making was considered an avocation as well as a trade — considered something to do that would occupy the mind as well as the fingers. It could teach useful fashion and household skills, and save the often enormous costs of buying it.

For well over three hundred years, lace-making in Western Europe constituted a major industry for a dozen countries. The work of some lace-making communities was prized as a national treasure and expert teachers were often in short supply to meet a growing need.

Against this background of need, together with a growing demand for ever-increasing varieties and quantities of lace production, the lace "school" emerged in the 1700s from what could only be called a "cottage industry" in earlier times. Lace schools were a way to accelerate the production of lace in order to have any hope of meeting rising demands. They also provided a way through which poor families could earn money. Their children could be sent to the school, kept busy learning necessary skills, and bring home the few coins that resulted from their labors.

In some communities, lace schools were to become so influential and numerous, that the areas in which they were situated became known as lace centers. Sprinkled throughout Europe, such centers and the schools from which they were formed, provided leadership in both innovation and style. The entire movement constituted a kind of glittering economic trajectory for the industry of lace-making all over Western Europe and established a new and unique role for the lace-maker in thousands of communities.

Experts were sought out. Some were bribed and imported from other countries to advance their art in a new and often subsidized setting. Quite literally, thousands of these lace makers were to establish new schools of their own and enjoy a level of social prominence equal to that of the "headmaster" or "headmistress."

Many hundreds of these lace schools relied entirely upon the labors of children. Both boys and girls were employed in various working conditions and environments. Some worked in an atmosphere as rigid as that of a convent and were kept strictly indoors to work on lace-making and spinning.

Records of these schools show that each working day was planned down to the minute. Often starting at four or five in the morning, the day typically began with an hour of pious exercises, prayers, or mass. By six in the morning, each child would begin working on their lace pieces — work that would continue until perhaps eight or ten o'clock at night, depending upon the child's age. Most days, these children would be grudgingly allowed to have a half hour away from their stools, pillows, bobbins, and needles, to stretch their cramped muscles and play. One meal each day was provided.

Many children, especially the older ones, would try to escape the rigors of the school, but they were closely watched and severely punished when caught. Records of one school in Northern Italy show that on June 16, 1743, the headmistress decided on yet another rule: "Any child who has deserted, without regard to her age, will be punished by fifteen days imprisonment, or more if it seems suitable. To discourage desertion in this school, punishment shall also include public whip-pings three times each day in the refectory."

Many lace schools were more like prisons or houses for the poor. Apprenticeships were conducted in harsh surroundings with discipline a constant presence. Work was always done in virtual silence and in an atmosphere of pious meditation, always with a duty to "submit to, respect, and obey your superiors."

Idle chatter while working was never permitted, but if a particular child had done an exceptional amount of work in a day, that child would be permitted to sing "suitable songs" as he or she worked the following day. "Suitability," however, was confined to songs about ever-increasing levels of production, of "fingers flying o'er the work," and "the blurring of bobbins passing in and through."

"Nineteen miles to the Isle of Wight,
Shall I be there by candle light?
Yes, if my fingers go lissome and light,
I'll be there by candle light.
There's three pins I done today,
What do you think my mother will say?
When she knows I done no more,
She'll take and turn me out of door,
Never let me come in any more."

Most lace schools dotting the Western European landscape employed about thirty to forty pupils with an average age that has been estimated at ten to eleven years old. Rooms were often small and confining. Work was often done in basements or at least in rooms without windows because direct sunlight could destroy the fine flaxen threads, turn linen cloths from snowy white to a tinged yellowish color, and allow too much heat into the room that might cause little hands to perspire and further ruin the work.

Each room containing the thirty or forty stools upon which the pupils sat to do their work was dominated by a teacher whose desk was often raised on a platform a foot or more above the floor. As mistress of all she surveyed, lace teachers invariably stayed within arm's reach of their ever-present canes or "scepters" — a symbol of their authority for over two hundred years — which rapped on the desk or floor to get attention, or worse.

Every hour, the teacher would move between the rows of students to inspect each pillow, and woe to the one who had not followed the pattern exactly, whose work was behind schedule for that hour, whose stitches were not drawn tightly enough, or whose behavior had drawn her attention in the first place.

The rustle of pins being placed would develop to a low murmur — each child trying to place more pins than a neighbor. At every tenth pin, the child could call out their number and to avoid teacher's wrath (and her cane), each was expected to place at least 600 pins in an hour. The clicking of the bobbins came next — reaching, twisting, braiding, under, over, and through — working on the threads stretched across the parchment patterns with the soft slipping sounds of wood on paper.

At the mealtime or when the day's toil was finally over, each child would carefully cover her own pillow, turn her four-legged stool over, and tuck the pillow gently between the legs of the stool to protect it through the night that had already long since begun.

Several generations of lacemakers often complained of headaches, dizziness, bent backs, eyestrain, and sore muscles from sitting in the required posture. Working in dark rooms before sunrise and often into the night could cause physical pain to become intense.

Typically, in the late of evening, younger children would be allowed to return to their homes or take to their beds in the school's dormitory. The older and more experienced pupils, however, would draw their stools around a few central candles or lantern and continue working until ten, eleven, or even midnight. In the records of one lace school in Ireland, the headmistress determined that "twelve is the number of workers that can accomplish their task in front of the light of one candle." Sitting in closely-arranged rows about the candle or lamp,

the least experienced could "sit nearest and can see. Them who sit in second light, can't see very well, and those of the third light must rely upon their skills to work in near darkness."

Problems only intensified for these lace makers when fashions turned to working with fine linen threads to produce black lace. In the dim light of the school rooms, work was often done entirely by touch "with a picture of the pattern etched in the mind" of the worker. In this way, the lacemaker had to quite literally "turn night into day" with imagination alone and the skills developed from years of hard-won experience.

It was not until the 1820s that some lace makers were protected under legislative controls. The First Report of the Children's Employment Commission, published in England in 1863, attempted to ameliorate child labor conditions and make the work more humane, but old practices continued almost without interruption until the late 1890s and even into the 20th Century.

Children, after all, could be taught at a very early age and would accept authority without the means to resist it. As lace-makers, children would at least have an occupation and the reward for their efforts could mean survival for not only them, but their entire families.

At a time when education was still the province of wealth and class, poor families believed that any learning is better than none at all. Lace schools provided a rare opportunity for the learning of a marketable skill, and as such, lacemaking was considered a prize that was not to be taken lightly.

"Look well to what you take in hand,
For learning is better than house or land;
When land is gone and money is spent,
Then learning is most excellent."
-Maggie Tulliver
"The Mill On The Floss"

Older than any lace school, however, was the patient work performed in the convents of Western Europe by the nuns. Only in convents, where time was of no consequence, was lace-

making studied as a separate artform and where only the most beautiful work was acceptable in the service of God.

Exquisite laces of the Vatican are often described in the history of lace. Fine work is still being made, displayed, and used in vestments, albs, stoles, dalmatics, cassocks, tunics, and chasubles. There are still some convents around the world continuing in the age-old traditions of lace-making in Spain, France, England, Ireland, and other European nations.

Filet Crochet, once known as "Nun's Work," is still being worked in convents today, as it has been for generations. Santa Florentina Convent, Spain.

Ecclesiastical needlework typical of the "Holy Point" that was worked in the convents throughout Western Europe during the Middle Ages. Santa Florentina Convent, Spain.

Ancient designs, faithful workmanship, and a devotion to produce only the finest patterns known to the world, characterize laces made in convents for the purposes of celebrating holy rites and special church observances.

Holy Point, or "Hollie" lace, can be traced back to the early Middle Ages and gradually became a generic term covering what we now classify as cut work, drawn work, darned netting, some embroideries, and needlepoint.

The various forms of needlework, including crochet, have often been called "Nun's Work." In their cloistered convents and churches throughout Spain, Italy, France, Yugoslavia, Ireland, Eastern Europe, and other remote areas throughout Western Europe, nuns designed and worked special laces with great care and devotion.

Using the simplest of materials such as fine cotton and linen threads, their work represents living examples of perfection in skilled craftsmanship, delicate colors, and varied styles that often precisely follow the design and colors of ancient paintings. Some of their embroidery pieces are so fine in their stitching that they appear to be extraordinary pieces of work done by a goldsmith rather than by one using a needle.

In fact, a main purpose of nuns in early times was to embroider, paint, and design their sacred articles with the most delicate touch of art that was either available to them or humanly possible for them to accomplish.

Since the Middle Ages, convent schools have long been part of the ecclesiastical tradition and years of academic, social, spiritual, and personal preparation for life included the needlecraft arts. Visiting their daughters in convent schools, many aristocratic noblemen offered magnificent gifts to the convents.

One such example is the Santa Florentina Convent founded during the Crusades in 1388 in the Andalucian Region of Spain. At first, it served as a sanctuary for women whose husbands had left them behind to fight in the Crusades.

A 15th Century Spanish nobleman offered a rare gift to that convent. He gave them his saddle blanket which was a beautifully embroidered piece with woven gold and silver. Later, the blanket was transformed into a dress for a doll that stands about thirty-five inches tall. This piece is representative of the well-developed form of needlework expression that existed in Spain.

Convents such as this one were considered quite wealthy during the 14th and 15th Centuries, and they were able to accumulate many thousands of pieces of exquisite laces and embroideries, often trimmed or made with gold and silver strands. The pieces were often tightly woven with floral designs and intricate embellishments which demonstrate the high degree to which the art of needlecraft had advanced within the confines of the convent walls.

In fact, the Santa Florentina Convent has documented its inventories since the year 1712. Record books and actual samples include early

Crochet Sample Book from the late 1800s. Santa Florentina Convent, Spain.

contain rich gold chalices with floral motifs and religious symbols that date back to ancient times. Often, the nuns copied the designs and complicated motifs from these ornate altar chalices into pieces of lace and carefully preserved them in long-forgotten drawers and sacristies.

Whether teaching the art of lace-making in the lace schools or in the convents, some sort of pattern or technique for design duplication was becoming increasingly necessary. Perhaps one or two in a hundred lace makers were also designers — people with the creative talent to take pen in hand and draw patterns from which other workers could form, stitch, and manipulate their laces.

Each piece made and sold was lost to these early designers. The parchments used to trace patterns were useless for the making of other works and increasingly, an urgent need developed — to produce patterns that lace-makers could duplicate, store, and use again. Further, as more and more workers were required to finish intricate pieces, fresh patterns and stitching instructions were needed in quantity.

Without a printing press in the early years of lace-making, pattern duplication became a very real and pressing chore. Each had to be hand-drawn in precise detail.

One of the very first pattern collections was to emerge in the year 1527 with some forty-two individual plates made from woodcut drawings. It was dupli-

Exquisite Cardinal's robe, embroidered with fine gold and silver during the early 19th Century. It is typical of the needlework done especially for ecclesiastical use in Zagreb. St. Stephen's Cathedral, Yugoslavia.

Crocheted cloth originally used as a priest's alb and worked by the nuns in a monastery near Zagreb. St. Stephen's Cathedral, Yugoslavia.

reticella and cut work, black and white laces, cloth pattern "books," and designs passed down through the centuries — testimonial treasures of the needlecraft art practiced since the Middle Ages.

On the eastern side of Europe, St. Stephen's Cathedral in Zagreb, Yugoslavia, is another example of the impressive inventories held by the Church. It maintains a treasury of outstanding pieces of lace and embroidery — worthy of "world-class" artistry in both design and accomplishment. Many fine embroideries made of silver and gold threads found here represent the tradition of needlework excellence.

Also in Yugoslavia, the 18th Century Church of St. Eustathius is home for an extensive collection of paintings by Croatian masters that document the various uses of lace and adornment in the area. There is a collection of lace from the 16th, 17th, and 18th Centuries from this same area which was known for its fine laces. The collection is representative of the thriving lace industry that existed throughout those centuries.

Lace-making along the rugged Yugoslavian coastline is well documented. The "Highway of the Adriatic" is still a well-traveled route along the inland seas, as it has been for thousands of years.

All over Europe there are examples of priests' robes and articles especially made for the Church and its "representatives" of God. They

Detailed close-up of the crochet design on a side altar in St. Mary's Church. Yugoslavia.

cated in the city of Cologne and contained stitching counts, designs for borders, and instructions for joining sections of the work together to make a complete design. Animal shapes and flowers were also detailed in these drawings.

Unable to meet a growing demand for new and different kinds of beautiful lace patterns, Pierre Quinty of Cologne published what is known in history as the first pattern book in the Catherine de Medici tradition — providing fresh ideas for the "arts done with a needle."

Frederico de Vinciolo, the designer and lace-maker from Venice who was moved to France by Catherine de Medici to provide her with her favorite Venetian laces, also succeeded in publishing many new designs or points for France.

Pattern books were very expensive and designers were limited in their ability to produce patterns in quantity. They soon found another avenue open to them — the making of "samplers" — as a demonstration of their work. Samplers first consisted of a collection of embroidery, lace, cut work, or drawn work on a foundation of coarse linen.

Sometimes these samples were called "Sam Cloths," and they were produced by designers to show how their ideas would look. Some of them were only a few square inches in size. Others were much larger in order to show how separate clusters, flowers, or particular arrangements could be incorporated into an overall concept. Some were over a yard long, eighteen inches wide, and embellished with their best ideas, and other demonstrations of their talents.

As designers presented themselves to their patrons to discuss a commission, they relied upon their "Sam Cloths" to speak for them. For the art and trade of lace-making, the importance of sam cloths or samplers cannot be underestimated. They were the means through which new ideas and innovations spread between lace centers, countries, and across continents. It was not until much later that pattern book publishing emerged as the common vehicle for lace commerce.

Later, samplers became a way for individuals to copy, practice, and preserve patterns for their own use and to share with friends and community.

"Punto in Aria" first appeared on a sampler made by Elizabeth Hinde in the year 1643, and the world has continued to appreciate her accomplishments ever since. She also produced samplers using damask patterns, "bird's

The Commemorative Crocheted Altar Cloth made by the women of St. Mary's Church to celebrate 500 years of existence for this parish in Pag. Yugoslavia.

eye" cut work, and drawn work in wide variety.

A common element included in the vast repertoire of designers making samplers was the alphabet worked in exotic geometric or flowery styles in the finest silks or white cotton.

Pattern book from the 1500s. Courtesy of the British Library.

On one sampler produced by Elizabeth Mackett before the turn of the 18th Century, a sense of her pride in accomplishment can be felt not only in the work she produced, but in a few lines of verse that she wrote to accompany it:

> *"When this you see, remember me*
> *And keep me in your mind,*
> *And be not like a weather rock*
> *That turns at every wind.*
> *When I am dead and laid in grave,*
> *And all my bones are rotten,*
> *By this you may remember me*
> *When I should be forgotten."*

Late in the 18th and into the early 19th Centuries, the invention and development of the machine gave new meaning to lace and lace production. "Old laces" belonged to the centuries past and "modern laces" signified the beginning of a new era in fashion that featured the lighter feel of the machinemade net. It was much less costly than the "old" handmade laces. The old lace makers tried to respond by using less expensive threads in their work, but the beautiful artistry of the lace suffered as a result.

Machinemade lace developed entirely by mechanical means, and it emerged fully with the birth of the Industrial Revolution during the 19th Century. For the first time in the history of lacemaking, there now existed a means to produce lace in quantity, and at a consistent level of quality. With machines, these first nets and tulles could indeed be produced for the masses in a bare fraction of the time it took to create it by hand, and at a cost everyone could afford to pay.

While machinemade lace was a coarse imitation of handmade lace, it was possible for everyone to own it, use it for personal adornment, and to add beautiful appointments and decor to their homes. This ability made them feel better about themselves and their yearnings to be fashionable.

However, very much like the unsuccessful

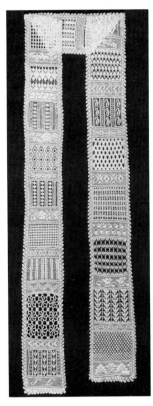

Crocheted samplers from the late 1800s. Courtesy of the New York Metropolitan Museum.

Luddites, who set out to smash all machines in an attempt to quash the Industrial Revolution, or for those today that believe automation is responsible for lost jobs and the decay of craftsmanship, the first lace-making machines introduced to the world caused an international controversy.

First attempts to replicate handmade laces through the use of mechanical devices were indeed

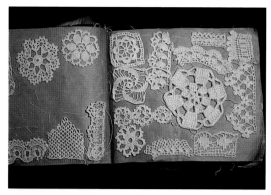

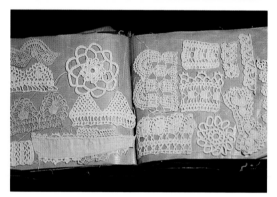

Pages from late 1800s crochet sampler book. Santa Florentina Convent, Spain.

crude. They lacked a true sense of style, and no doubt caused desultory whispers throughout the entire industry. But machines were quickly developed and made to produce in a few hours or days what used to require months or even years by hand. Many professional lace-makers probably began to wonder in amazement, "What hath God wrought!"

History records that the first primitive machine net appeared in 1763 and led to the beginnings of machinemade nets —the backing for all kinds of laces. Many historians of lace-making have concluded the ability to produce netting quickly and completely by machine changed the art forever.

Frames fashioned first of wood and then of metal, were at the leading edge of mechanization in the lace arts. A stocking frame was made by John Hammond in 1760 to produce what became known as "single press point." His frame punched holes in a backing fabric to increase the speed of working that material with needles and bobbins.

Fifteen years later, several inventors in England produced the first warp-frame used essentially for weaving. The frame caused a sensation throughout Europe. By 1785, the warp-frame enjoyed such popularity that improvements were made on it so that it could be used not only for weaving, but also for knitting. With each passing decade, weaving and knitting frames were built that quite literally doubled the speed of operation. Larger frames were devised, and by the

year 1800, frames were working on materials up to forty-four inches wide and doing it at incredible speeds; a feat unheard of before that time.

Not surprisingly, less than a decade passed until a first bobbin net frame was invented by John Heathcote in Tiverton, England. Combining the warp methods used for knitting frames with threads from bobbins made to pass across and link into the warp, his patents and early factory at Loughborough attracted attention throughout Europe.

Mr. Heathcote's achievement led others to refine the bobbin principles he used, create mechanized workturns, and apply machines to the tatting industry. Warp tatting then rode the crest of popularity and quite literally hundreds of new machines were manufactured. Schools of design were formed around these machines and students came from far and wide to learn techniques of using them to produce "imitation laces" that were often criticized as little more than a passing "fad."

In Nottingham, warp-tatting machines created a whole new industry. Pieces of wearing apparel such as scarves, capes, shawls, caps, blouses, and hundreds of other pieces were turned out at a fraction of what these same items had previously cost. Many of them were completed entirely by machines. Others added handmade embroideries, or other touches of distinctive ornamentation.

In less than twenty-five years, thousands of machines for textile production were operating throughout Western Europe. They turned out imitations of nets, blond edgings, and miles of imitation thread laces. Clever machines and their operators turned out more work in a day or two than armies of lace-makers could have produced in several years.

Until the machine age, lace was a treasure that could be enjoyed only by the very rich. Royalty. The aristocracy. Each owner buying and wearing it as a symbol of culture and rank. Now, however, anyone could easily acquire "lace" curtains, all manner of "lace-trimmed" clothing, and "lace-like" appointments for the household. The consequence of availability spelled the irretrievable demise of the handmade lace industry as it had been known and revered for centuries.

With the improvement of machinemade lace, old designs and techniques could be duplicated with exactness and precision. Buyers soon had difficulty distinguishing between handmade lace and machinemade lace pieces. Prices fell.

One 19th Century critic commented that, "...Machines first spelled doom for the careless, bad worker in lace. Machines could now produce bad laces much faster and cheaper." And so they did — around the clock, week in and week out, year after year — flooding world markets with a flourish and forever ending the now discouraged and frustrated pillow-lace industry — all this change in the space of a few incredible years.

At one time, the lace-maker could be paid thousands of dollars for a single piece of hand made lace; where quite literally hundreds of thousands were spent on a special wedding gown; where years slowly passed as orders were being filled; where at several times in history there were a million and more lace-makers actively working the trade. Now, in the Industrial Age, a single factory worker could easily handle several machines in an almost effortless posture and turn out vast quantities with the turn of handles, levers, and drive mechanisms.

Inevitably, there were social consequences. Machines in the lace-making industries often caused some disastrous effects on lifestyle for both men and women. Work previously done essentially in the home, now moved to noisy factories in the main cities of virtually every country in Western Europe. Lace-making centers once situated in many of those larger communities could no longer compete and ceased to exist. Lace schools gradually wound down their production, dismissed their pupils, and closed their doors. Many of them set aside their bobbins, pins, and pillows to give way to the teaching of reading, writing, and arithmetic. The social order changed — almost

within the blinking of an eye — and a new age had come with a whole new set of requirements, adaptations, and wonders. Many people of the wealthy classes still treasured the laces that their fortunes had assembled from the earlier days and still proudly displayed them at social gatherings. Cheaper, machinemade versions had diminished the value and pride of wearing lace. The machine

Lace pattern from 1544. Courtesy of the Victoria and Albert Museum.

Lace pattern from 1544. Courtesy of the Victoria and Albert Museum.

managed to damage the lace industry in a way that wars, revolution, edicts, or church policy had never done in past centuries. Making lace by hand, an artistic and creative profession and a source of personal pride for the owner, had become for all practical purposes, a dying art in this new age.

The Volart Encajes Y Tejidos, S.A., is a

Honiton Lace made on machine made net in 1865. Courtesy of the Victoria and Albert Museum.

factory typical of the lace factories that were common in Cataluna, Spain during the 19th Century Industrial Revolution. Five generations of the same family have been dedicated to the development, production, and commercialization of lace. The first preserved documents from 1856 indicate that the factory was then dedicated to the manufacture of handmade lace. The enterprise was born through the efforts of D. Ricardo Campmany and D. Casimiro Volart e Ibern.

Years later, the two separated and the business was continued by Volart with the help of his sons Juan and Ramon. In the beginning, the Volarts lived on the first floor of the family factory. The family maintained the business and responded to modern change with expansion and new locations.

At the beginning of the 20th Century, Ramon Volart imported the first Leaver lace machines from England. The factory became known all over Spain for the production of mach-

inemade lace. At that time, those machines were the most advanced in existence.

Those who sold the machines to this Spanish factory doubted that their full potential would ever be realized. A French phrase lamented that there "was too much sun in Spain." In reality, these machines caused the birth of the industrial production of lace in Spain.

Under the direction of D. Ramon Volart Costa, the factory was able to acquire twenty-four machines of this type along with a workforce of nearly two hundred people having the proper qualifications and technological background.

In 1935, the company adopted its present name, Volart Encajes Y Tejidos, S.A., and D. Ramon was the first president under the new name. After his death, his son-in-law, D. Jose M. Estany Jemena became president.

During the latter part of the 1950s a synthetic fiber appeared on the market that opened up the possibilities to produce lace on Ketten and

Wooden punch cards from the old leaver lace machines used during the early 20th Century. Volart Encajes Y Tejidos, S.A., Spain.

Ketten and Raschel lace-making machine used during the late 1950s. Volart Encajes Y Tejidos, S.A., Spain.

Lace production on the computerized, state of the art Jacquard system presently being used. Volart Encajes Y Tejidos, S.A., Spain.

In its one hundred and thirty years of existence, this factory has survived two world wars, a civil war, many political changes, and fluctuating economic conditions of all kinds. Overcoming these obstacles, the factory is successfully moving into the next century.

Raschel machines. This added a new dimension to the development of the Spanish lace industry.

Also, during this same period, and coinciding with the entrance of the fourth generation of the Volart family into the business, a new factory was built in 1957. Since that time, this has been the only factory in Spain that is capable of producing lace in both versions, Leaver and Raschel.

Then, under the direction of the fifth generation Volart, Ramon Estany Bufill, who was also an industrial engineer, the factory integrated its C.E.E. system with the first machines of the Raschel system and with seventy-eight electronic bars of the Jacquard system. Technologically, this represents the most advanced lace production system to be found anywhere in the world.

The current president, D. Ramon Estany Volart, is also very active in the European committee of lace manufacturers seated in Paris. This factory has also won many awards of distinction

A fifth generation member of the Volart family to be involved in the production of lace in Spain presents a traditional Spanish Mantilla to Annie, the author.

for its lace production and consistent contributions to the lace industry since 1864.

Machinemade lace was possible through all of these changes brought about by the great Industrial Revolution in Europe. New technologies made it possible to quickly, easily, and inexpensively, imitate the handmade laces of earlier centuries. For essentially the same reasons, crochet was developed to rapidly become a distinctive and creative needleart that could also be used to copy the revered classic laces.

The roots of crochet as a technique for the making of clothing and other personal articles can be traced back across many generations along with other textile arts such as netting, braiding, weaving, knitting, and lace-making. Some say that decorative crochet evolved directly from the art of tambour because of the hooked needle and the chain stitch that are common to both. The "modern" art of true crochet, as we know it today, was developed during the 16th Century. It became known as "crochet lace" in France and "chain lace" in England.

Early crochet clearly drew its inspiration from older needlecrafts as well as from other textile influences of Italy, Spain, Greece, Turkey, Egypt, Yugoslavia, and many other countries. In early centuries, references to crochet are vague and speculative at best. These early chain or "cheyne" laces often used metals and silk to produce clothing and other household decorations using braids, loops, or knots.

Chain laces are a bridge between ancient and modern forms of the art of crochet. References to some of the earliest techniques of chain lace in England, for example, include bedding "garnished with a cheyne lace of goulde and silver-copper" that was owned by the Earl of Leicester in the 1560s at Kenilworth Castle.

Among the prized possessions of Queen Elizabeth I, who ruled England between 1558 and 1603, was a "gowne that was exquisitely laid aboute with small cheyne laces of gold." The description of such garments made with "crochet chains" connected by slip stitches are all examples that help to document the path of the develop-

ment of crochet. They shed light on the beginnings of this very special craft and help unravel the mystery of its origins.

Elizabeth had a special love of fine clothes, gowns, and accessories. She commissioned only the most talented lacemakers to produce her imposing wardrobe, and artisans were constantly seeking out creative new ideas for their designs in order to please her. These innovators used ancient techniques of craftsmanship and tools to create exquisite new looks and unknowingly constructed a course of needlecraft history that would eventually lead to the explosion of crochet as a separate artform that was to sweep across the world.

Queen Elizabeth had a number of gowns, capes, and accessories that were made with "knot work done with a chainstitch and bound with tape made of nun's thread." While such pieces could also mean that they were made using netting techniques, these descriptions of her wardrobe inventory accurately describe crochet net work and "chain lace." Could such pieces made with a chained arrangement of loops, knots, and openwork design have been produced without the use of the hooked instruments that were widely used during the 16th Century throughout Western Europe and the surrounding regions? Were these hooked instruments descendants of those discovered in the excavations of the ancient (7th to 10th Centuries) Frigian cities of Gordion and Midas in the Anatolian region of Turkey?

The "nun's thread" in Queen Elizabeth's inventory is terminology that refers to the well documented "Nun's Work" as was practiced at the time in cloistered convents and churches throughout Europe. Crochet and other forms of needlework were steadily refined and worked to perfection by these cloistered nuns.

Exercising patience as a virtue, they took the time to examine the intricacies of stitches, motifs, patterns, and to create fresh ideas. Devoted nuns worked outstanding pieces of ecclesiastical designs for altar cloths, albs, and other religious items.

An exploration of some ancient cathedrals, sacristies, and convents can uncover rare pieces of crochet that have been long forgotten and

Queen Elizabeth I, wearing a lace trimmed gown from her fabulous wardrobe. Courtesy of the National Portrait Gallery, London.

quietly folded into drawers, trunks, and vaults. Most of these pieces are breathtaking in their simplicity of design. Perfectly preserved, many of the pieces are awe-inspiring. In all of them, there is an obvious dedication to both tradition and a freshness of style that can be instantly recognized.

Making no attempt to produce crochet pieces for commercial profit, the quiet traditions of

the art have been maintained for centuries by these dedicated hands. Each piece has a story behind it. Who made it? How long did it take her? What was she thinking as she carefully selected the material? Did she teach others? How? Was her activity as satisfying to her as the art she created was to those who enjoyed it?

Ecclesiastical crochet represents a high standard of technique and beauty. Dresses, capes, shawls, caps, marriage gowns, christening robes for infants, gloves, runners, tablecloths, altar mantles, and thousands of other exquisitely produced articles of crochet can be seen and appreciated as a tribute to the nuns who advanced and perpetuated the art and history of crochet.

It is true that "...by their works ye shall know them" and the nuns who helped to perfect the artistic and lasting values of crochet shall never be forgotten. Their faith, love of beauty, and determination to elevate their skills and creative genius of their minds will continue to inspire others for generations to come.

Crochet work done in the convents of Europe often imitated expensive laces and embroideries because they were so beautiful and revered. To the dedicated nun, the skills of crochet were a gift from God, and their work would become a tangible testimony to the faith and love that they wanted returned to the Church. Theirs was a work of their hands — worthy of symbolizing their marriage to God.

Through it, they could demonstrate in a magnificent outward way the dedication of their life to Him. For many of them, crochet became an interpretation of inner beauty that they could use to enhance the mystery of ritual and of the church. Creating beauty, for all ages and all people, has been a way to create a sense of perfection.

Because nuns were often engaged in missionary work, they could have easily spread their skills in the crochet arts to many other countries along with their faith. Since crochet only requires a ball of thread and a needle, it was easy to learn and easy to carry anywhere.

The versatility of the craft made it possible to create and copy an endless number of textile patterns. A single piece of crochet could hold any number of styles from the "lace influence" and there was a variety of techniques pos-

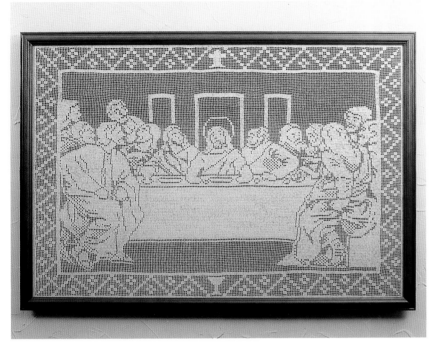

Filet Crochet picture depicting "The Last Supper."

sible for crochet that would have boggled the mind of a traditional lace-maker.

Further, crochet required less attention when counting stitches than most other needlecrafts, and it was probably done simultaneously while praying, talking, singing, or meditating. Also opposed to other needlecrafts, crochet could be easily unraveled to correct a mistake.

It was the nuns in a convent located in the city of Rouen, for example, who have been credited with developing a new form of "filet crochet," a style that later became known worldwide as "Square-Stitched Crochet." Nuns used this technique to crochet a copy of the painting of Da Vinci's "Last Supper" — a style for crochet that is both classical and traditional.

The nuns of France became famous for teaching the art of crochet to the daughters of the wealthy who attended their convent schools as if they were "finishing" schools. Gradually, crochet became an expected skill if a young girl was to be considered as "well born" in society.

One such lady was Eleonore Riego De La Branchardiere, a name that will be forever linked to the heritage of Irish and English needlepoint arts. She devoted her life in the 19th Century to the same ideals of innovative beauty and design that had been nurtured in the convents for generations.

She was born in England to a father of Franco Spanish nobility, and an Irish mother. The family was driven from France during the height of the French Revolution, a time when thousands of aristocrats lost their lives to the guillotines; a time when Paris had grown accustomed to the sound of death; a time when thousands more were to seek escape or be executed.

Because of her Irish ancestry, Mlle. Riego was uncommonly determined to make the conditions of life better for the Irish peasantry by helping to develop new ideas, designs, and marketing for the entire Irish crochet industry. Her patronage and creative leadership survived her death in 1887, and indeed, continues to this day through her Branchardiere Fund in Dublin. Her generous spirit has provided help, encouragement, and financial support for individual excellence in the lace and crochet industries of Ireland for the past hundred years.

Mlle. Riego devoted her life to her profession and its artistic expression. Following an "avant-garde" career style for women of her day, this extraordinary lady is known as a creative needlewoman, an accomplished crochet designer, a teacher of commoners as well as royalty, and a prolific writer and publisher.

Even in her day, when women were rarely acknowledged for leadership roles either in society or in business, she was recognized as an authority

86 *Mlle. Eleonore Riego de la Branchardiere, leading 19th Century crochet designer and publisher. From the personal collection of the author.*

in crochet, knitting, tatting, and lacework. She knew the fashions as well as the politics of her times. She conversed easily with the Royal Courts of a half-dozen countries. She was shrewd and calculating as a business executive. She knew people. Her tireless energies stimulated her profession and her standards continue to this day.

Mlle. Riego is perhaps best known for her ability to imitate and richly enhance the lace of ancient times and to then offer clear instructions on how to duplicate them. Her pattern books are filled with beautifully engraved designs and easily understood illustrations. She, perhaps more than any other individual in history, had the means and the creative capacity to make the art of beautiful crochet possible for millions of people.

With her education and artistic dedication as a designer, she understood the principles of beauty and graceful lines. She was familiar with antique laces, as well as with exceptional works of fine art, architecture, and design. With her creative mind, technical proficiency, and hooked needle, she took crochet out of its cloistered traditions and brought it into international visibility. To her, the essence of creativity was something that was not only useful, but that was also aesthetically beautiful.

In 1848, the Leicester Journal recognized her books "to be among the most useful and cheapest" that were available to guide and stimulate the needlepoint arts. As an original designer, Mlle. Riego was awarded the only Prize Medal at the Great Exhibition of 1851 "...for Crochet, Point, and Point Lace." Hers was recognized as the first true example of Irish Crochet. Her achievements and recognition helped immeasurably to push crochet into the international limelight as a form of creative and artistic expression. Her designs and individual efforts also received Medals for Excellence in 1855, 1862, and 1872.

In each instance where her work achieved national or international acclaim, judges made special note of her simple, yet exquisite style and design — a mark of true brilliance.

Before Mlle. Riego's publications, older pattern books had been passed from house to house between crochet workers and consisted largely of actual samples of stitches that were sewn directly onto a cotton or parchment page.

Each user of these pattern books studied the samples, picked out one that they would try, and attempted to duplicate it by eye and their skills of hand. No real instructions were provided in the books.

With Mlle. Riego's publications, however, samples were completely illustrated with step-by-step instructions that formed a "How To" plan to guide every stitch. Her written instructions inspired crochet workers everywhere and her pattern books were quickly circulated to become a standard in a new and developing home industry. No longer dependent upon the experience or long-developed skills of the worker, more consistent results could be produced in the crochet art.

An early publication, "The Queen," reported that "with Mlle. Riego's directions, we may always feel safe and when they are illustrated, we

Front cover of the magazine, "The Needle," one of the first major needlecraft periodicals to be published. Mid 1800s. Courtesy of The British Museum

Isabella del Sera, wearing a 17th Century Collar. This represents a lace design which is similar to the collar that Mlle. Riego later copied in crochet.
88 *Courtesy of the Uffizi Gallery.*

RAISED SPANISH POINT
COLLAR?

PRIZE MEDAL, PARIS, 1855.

Engraving of the Raised Spanish Point Collar designed by Mlle. Riego during the 19th Century.

may rest secure that the piece of work in hand will not bring disappointment with completion."

Eleonore Riego De La Branchardiere quickly became known throughout the Continent as a designer without equal. Her most significant contribution was not solely in her designs, however, but was in the fact that once having completed a piece, she had the talent to break a design down into a set of easily-followed instructions that others could understand and duplicate. Her many hundreds of pattern books stimulated the art of crochet among literally millions of people, young and old, who could successfully reproduce the designs she offered and experience for themselves the pride that comes from being able to turn out beautiful crochet pieces in an incredible variety.

Leafing through collections of Mlle. Riego's pattern books, the common themes are usefulness, making gifts for others that would be treasured for their simple beauty, and using crochet as a productive yet leisurely activity.

From 1852 to 1854, in her periodical publication called "The Needle," Mlle. Riego wrote detailed instructions for her designs along with recommendations on what materials to use that "would make a lady's work table complete." She began her business enterprise to protect herself from what had become flagrant piracy of her designs.

Increasingly, she also wanted to provide the kind of help to the waiting thousands of women who were trying to make a living from their needlework, as well as to help people who wanted to use crochet at home for their own amusement.

Important to Mlle. Riego's motivations was the fact that she also wanted to raise needlework to the level of an artform in its own right. For her, crochet was a way to capture history in

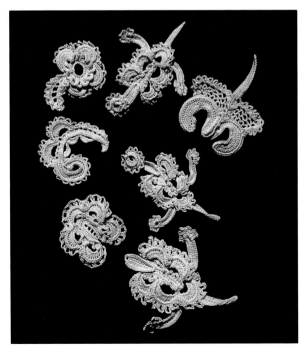

Motifs crocheted from Mlle. Riego's pattern of the Raised Spanish Point Collar.

needlework. Her publications included designs of historical importance that would represent a variety of periods and styles such Arabian, Saracenic, Turkish, Gothic, Classical, Medieval, Renaissance, Elizabethan, and mixed modern.

Mlle. Riego was interested in designs that were representative of different cultures and also those that held special historical significance. She was able to recognize important designs and motifs and incorporate them into her work.

Through her publications, she also sought out suggestions among her readers for their design ideas. A typical invitation is found in her publication of June, 1852, where she wrote, "I particularly invite communications on all subjects connected with the Needle, as it will always be a pleasure to receive suggestions from correspondents for new designs, or any matter calculated to lead to an improvement of the Art...I have only to add that my best endeavors to fulfill the arduous task I have undertaken, shall be given to render my magazine worthy of public support in connection with the ornamental portions of needlework..."

She solicited ideas for new patterns and the best work from her many readers. She became one of the most-loved promoters and teachers of the crochet arts in her time.

In 1886 she wrote, "As I have always had the desire to assist those who by their skill and industry can use their needle as a means of obtaining a livelihood, it gave me great pleasure to hear of the noble efforts now being made to revive the productions of the poor Irish workers, in whom I have ever taken a deep interest..." She published some of her best designs for this cause and explained how her readers could create valuable lace at a small cost with popular designs. Her patterns consistently held to the themes of usefulness and purpose. They were practical and of enduring quality, as opposed to designs that would merely cater to the changing whims of fashion. She believed that crochet lace was her own invention.

Mlle. Riego wrote, "I may claim that all this class of work owes its origin to my early books,

as crochet lace did not exist before the publication of my first one on that subject which appeared in 1846, about the time of the dreadful famine in Ireland." She supported their cause and became a means through which Irish Crochet Lace was to reach international importance in world markets.

She is known to have worked closely with her pattern book readers. Mlle. Riego was a new and respected designer. She offered fresh ideas. Her reputation as a teacher was growing. But, her real fame came to her as a result of her ability to translate even the most complex of designs into easily-followed instructions that she published for her rapidly growing number of readers.

Many of Mlle. Riego's designs were inspired by old exquisite laces that she knew from years of appreciation and study. She was particularly intrigued by the antique raised Spanish Point Lace and as a child, wanted to revive that ancient art. In July of 1886, Mlle. Riego wrote:

"The raised Spanish Point, although now produced by a modern art, is a copy of a valuable specimen of this ancient lace, and formerly belonged to the Marquise de M___, one of the Dames de la Cour to Marie Antoinette; this lady when young suffered severely during the Revolution, her first husband being executed. By his wish that she might not bear his name, she at once married his friend the Vicomte de C___, but in a few weeks he also lost his life and then for some time she made shirts for the Republican soldiers at three sous each, and in after years often said she was thankful she had learnt to use her needle, as her working not only gave her the means of existence, but enabled her to conceal her rank, and was thus the means of saving her life.

"It was this Lace that gave me the idea when quite a child to try and revive the work, then said to be a lost art; but after conquering the original mode of making it, I found I could produce a similar effect with my crochet needle, the advantages of crochet being that it was worked in a quarter of the time, and that I could write more exact instructions for others to make it. For

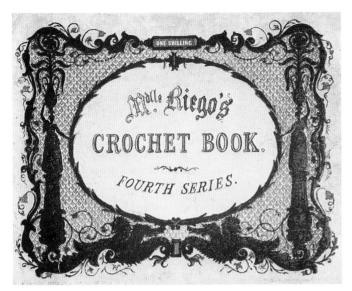

Front Cover of a pattern book published by Mlle. Riego. Courtesy, The Austin Library.

the former method, there must be a drawn outline of the pattern, in some cases designed by the greatest painters, and even when the various stitches were learnt there was no rule how to apply them, a knowledge only acquired by long practice and artistic skill.

"With the accompanying directions, needle, thread, and an amateur knowledge of Crochet, the lace can be successfully reproduced, but to write instructions for such designs is a task of patient study, the present one having taken five years of spare time to perfect during which period, however, it obtained two prize medals, also a third, when arranged in a more elaborate form, for an altar Frontal..."

Mlle. Riego was also responsible for the revival of antique geometric Greek patterns that were very popular in Paris in the mid-19th Century. She created arrangements of crochet patterns to reproduce antique effects. Her engravings of Greek Point were copied from ancient designs which she then adapted to her own patterns. Greek Point Lace was one of the earliest forms of all lace and was later known as "Reticella," sometimes called "Venetian Guipure."

One of Mlle. Riego's early publications, titled "Knitting, Crochet, and Netting with Illustrations," was produced in 1846. By command of Queen Victoria in 1887, she also published the "Royal Jubilee Crochet Book." Many of her best designs are found in this important publication.

In a letter to a close friend, she wrote, "...it seems strange to me to be again designing for the Court. My first knitting was for the Queen's Mother, her late Majesty's Duchess of Kent. After teaching all her granddaughters, and writing over one hundred books, I am able to make her Daughter's Jubilee lace."

Mlle. Riego also designed instructions for a Royal Banner Screen in crochet applique for flags and other decorations. She claimed to have invented crochet applique as a substitute for embroidery for large pieces that must be visible at a distance. She also described her opportunity to influence baby fashions when she created the Berceaunette Cover for the royal infant, Duke of Clarence, and the Point Lace Cap used for christenings and other special occasions. For this latter work, she copied a baby hat once worn by George III, by blending crochet with point lace.

With amazing success for her time, Mlle. Riego reached international fame. She had an intuitive sense of marketing and was able to work out business arrangements with textile mills, suppliers of yarns in a variety of weights, and importers of rare threads from throughout the world.

Scarf with the traditional Greek Reticella lace. National Historic Museum, Greece.

Her fame spread steadily. Princess Collamaki took Mlle. Riego's books to Turkey and spent years teaching the Turkish women how to make flowers in crochet. Her files began to fill with letters from readers in Germany, Italy, Poland, Prussia, and England who requested more pattern books from her and who praised her designs published as a result of her research and observation. Some

Author's crocheted copy of Greek Reticella lace.

asked for more detailed accounts of her appointments and the lessons that she gave to members of British Royalty.

A Certificate of Merit was presented to Mlle. Riego in 1871 for successfully instructing the blind. One completely blind lady worked a point lace alb and Benediction Veil for the Pope, and requested more designs from Mlle. Riego for religious pieces.

Orris Lace was introduced by Mlle. Riego in 1886, and is a variation worked with a crochet hook using gold, silk, and wool threads with interwoven beads. Orris was her invention. It was a lightweight, unique, and fairly inexpensive lace, considering that gold threads were featured. It was the same type of gold thread especially made for this particular kind of needlework   she had used years earlier for ecclesiastical embroideries.

Cornelia Mee was an early 19th Century English designer who also claimed to be the inventor of crochet lace. She was born in Bath, England,

Crocheted Oyas from Turkey.

to a father who was an undertaker and haberdasher, and to a mother of German descent. Her mother and father died early, and by the age of fourteen, Cornelia was an orphan along with the six other children in her family.

She and her husband, Charles, operated a needlework shop and there she wrote her first and most important work, the "Manual of Knitting, Netting, and Crochet," first published in 1842.

She also published other booklets dealing mainly with crochet, between 1842 and 1847, such as her 1847 work titled "Coubrettes and Collars." She and her sister prepared these works which included instruction manuals as well as books. One, "The Worktable Magazine," was a monthly series. Mee's writings explored crochet and its new possibilities for the use of the needle.

In her book titled "Bijou Receipts for Baby's Wardrobe," she wrote, "... nothing being known till she published her first book on crochet, but the common shepherd's crook crochet."

The Mees continued to be successful, and by 1858, Cornelia, her husband, and her sister had moved their business to one of the most fashionable districts in London. There, she also continued to publish books on crochet and became involved with many pressing social concerns of the day. She wrote:

"So many applications have been made for rules for making warm things for the poor of Lancashire, this little book has been hastily arranged in an inexpensive form to meet the wishes of any benevolent ladies who are occupying their time working for the distressed operatives."

All of Mee's patterns were for useful household pieces. None of them could be labeled "frivolous," or calculated to ride current fads for fashion. She has long been considered a major contributor to English crochet and knitting through a productive career of more than thirty years.

Other early publishers of note during the late 19th Century include Jane Gaugain of Edinburgh, who in 1836 published "The Lady's Assistant for Executing Useful and Fancy Designs in Knitting, Netting, and Crochet Work." In 1840, she also published a work in England without illustrations, and another work in 1842 that included drawings and pictures.

She explained her publications as a "means of affording a genteel and easy source of livelihood to many well-disposed and industrious females..." and also described the tone of her publications as, "... not only a book of fashionable amusement to the higher ranks of society..."

Frances Lambert was also published in England during this time period. Her work, "Handbook of Needlework," was typical of other needlework publications of the day which sought aristocratic patronage and approval. These publications also encouraged needleworkers to maintain a formal manner, high moral standards, and dedication to the service of God throughout their lives.

This attitude was characteristic of England during that time, the "Victorian Age" — the time when Queen Victoria ruled (1837-1901). Those were the years when England was developing a strong colonial Empire. Queen Victoria and her husband, Prince Albert, played strong roles in that development.

She was devoted to Albert and learned much about the duties of royalty from him. When she first met him, she wrote in her diary, "It was with some emotion that I beheld Albert — who is beautiful."

Beauty of another kind was also very important to Queen Victoria. Her love of crochet lace was an important element in the popularization of the art among the nobility and the aristocracy. She once accepted a gift of the famous Irish crochet and as a result Irish crochet quickly became extremely popular among the wealthy of England. Members of the English aristocracy were always anxious to acquire the latest crochet rose point. Gifts of crochet were often given to wealthy women and royalty in exchange for favors.

Queen Victoria herself learned to crochet. In fact, it was this peaceful and relaxing activity that helped her to cope with her grief after the death of her beloved Albert. Her daughters were also known to make crochet pieces as gifts to be given at Christmas and birthdays to family members.

"Victorian" crochet as a separate style followed the example set by the Irish and was done in very fine cotton threads made to resemble antique laces. It became widely used for everything such as covering furniture, making pantaloons, doilies, table mats, cushion covers, camisole tops, and even the covering of piano legs.

Into the 20th Century, English crochet maintained the look of the Victorian Age. Pieces such as collars, tablecloths, and gloves were still trimmed in Victorian-style crochet. Antimacas-

Queen Victoria crocheting, 1889. Reproduced by gracious permission of Her Majesty Queen Elizabeth II.

sars were used to protect chair backs from oily heads long after oily hair fell out of fashion. The practice of using cheval and duchess sets to protect dressing tables from spilled colognes and lotions continued for years.

Besides Irish Crochet, hairpin, broomstick, and filet crochet became very popular techniques. Filet crochet makes it possible to produce pictures and abstract designs within a fabric. Mlle. Riego had set the pace for this style and many publications for design patterns and other information on needlework flourished. One of the most important publishers was Weldon, who produced "Weldon's Practical Needlework," from 1886 to 1893. From 1936 to 1939, it became "Weldon's Series." Many issues were devoted to crochet. He also published "Weldon's Fashion Series," "Weldon's New Crochet Series," and "Weldon's Beautiful Needlework." His other works included a hard-cover book called "Weldon's Practical Shilling Guide to Fancy Work" — later to become "Weldon's Needlework Encyclopedia."

Another important publisher of the era was Mrs. Clara Leach. Beginning in 1886, and through subsequent years, she produced "Mrs. Leach's Ladies Work and Crochet," "Leach's Sixpenny Series," and "Leach's Home Needlework."

In France during 1886, Therese de Dillmont published the "Encyclopedia of Needlework," which was translated into English, German, Italian, and Spanish. In later years, it became known as the "bible" among many needleworkers. She also built upon Mlle. Riego's foundation of ideas and elaborated on a process already well-known. At the Chicago Exhibition of 1893, her book was considered to be among the "most useful in women's education."

Around the world, many talented and creative crochet designers were publishing books and manuals with detailed instructions. Design itself, as originally stressed by Mlle. Riego, was becoming an increasingly critical element in these creations. What inspired the endless variety of design, from the bold to the delicate to the mysterious? Design that could symbolize power, splendor, and wealth to the world? What inspired the beauty that could be created from the work of the hand with a simple ball of thread and a hooked needle? Did Riego and other designers intend their work to be a gift of beauty that could be shared by future generations?

Obviously, they were aware of the beauty in their environment and in nature. Flowers, trees, leaves, animals, insects, palm trees, cypress, dates, figs, pomegranates, grapevines, and other elements of nature have been copied into adornment patterns for clothing since ancient times. Often, they were used to symbolize eternal life, growth, fertility, abundance, and prosperity.

Some would say that the popular pineapple crochet pattern may have had its roots in the ancient symbolism of the pine tree and its pine cone. For the ancient Arabs, that symbol has been

a way of representing everlasting life. That pattern is still called the "tree of life" in Turkey today.

The ancient Greeks also revered the pine tree, and ancient legends speak of it as being a source of renewed energy and strength. It was always planted near the olive tree, itself a symbol of grace and culture. It was believed that together, the pine and the olive tree produced a balance with nature — for the enduring values of civilization. Designers also copied patterns from everyday items such as the pattern of brick laid within old cobblestone streets. The design of the tile pattern that has been used to pave important streets in the Andalucian region of Spain, particularly Cadiz, is one example. The pattern is called "alargarbia," meaning uproar. It uses a geometric paving stone of curved and mesh lines that have often been copied into lace and crochet patterns.

Every nation of every age has witnessed the creation of magnificent architecture — marvelous cathedrals and palaces that quite literally were prayers or poetry "in stone" — built to

Crocheted grapes from Yugoslavia.

Pineapple crochet design. Courtesy of Annie's Attic.

glorify God, or often the royalty who would reside there. The design motifs, glass work, marble and grill work often associated with these buildings inspired confidence, power, and beauty among the people. Crochet and other needlework designers copied what they saw in these magnificent buildings. They felt that the splendor of beautiful architecture could daily enrich the homes of everyone when recreated in a piece of crochet work.

The Alhambra Palace is an outstanding example of architectural magnificance. It looms large on the horizon above Granada, Spain and is regarded as the finest example of Moorish architecture in the world. Built in the 13th Century, the name for this fortress comes from the Arabic word meaning "The Red" — because there is an amber glow from its walls. Also, during its construction, thousands of workers toiled through the long nights working under the often mysterious reddish glow of their torches.

Here, in ancient times, the people of the region were called "Mauri" by the Romans, or "Moors." They were also called "Berbers," with roots imbedded deeply into the cultures of Northwestern Africa. They and the Moslems dominated the entire civilization in this part of the world for nearly a thousand years.

Despite its size — covering thirty-five acres with tiled floors, arched walkways, rhombic decorations, open-work designs, marble columns, reflecting pools, and thirteen towers stretching toward the heavens — the Alhambra has been a legendary meeting place for kings and queens — the royalty of the world — for hundreds of years.

Today, a visitor strolling through the expansive rooms, graceful patios, terraces, and gardens, cannot help but feel the majesty and incomparable beauty of the Alhambra's history. Alabaster, filigree, polichromed tiles, mosaics, and the splendor of vaulted ceilings and arched balconies provide a heady mixture of fantasy and reality.

To the student of crochet, lace, architecture, art, and other handicrafts, the Alhambra itself is a study in exquisite design. Nearly ten cen-

turies of Moslem influence has marked this place as the beginning of a new Renaissance in the arts. It reflects of a culture that bridged ancient with modern times in the vast Mediterranean Region.

Here, ceramic works deeply etched with primitive and traditional shapes, embellished with deep blues, greens, and purples are molded to plaster, inlaid woods, ivory, and mother of pearl. Basic to the motifs used in Moorish designs and in splendid evidence at the Alhambra,

Stone lace curtains carved into the Alhambra Palace during the 13th Century. Spain.

are the branches, trunks, and leaves of trees. The importance of motifs is often symbolic in nature. These designs are able to draw on the unconscious and to express what is in the soul of man toward his desire for eternal life.

Continuity of patterns through generations tells of an ageless desire for immortality. All of these impressions, human passions, and cultural beliefs can be found in the

A crochet design inspired by the stone lace curtains in the Alhambra Palace.

architecture and decor of the Alhambra.

In this emotionally charged atmosphere, the Moorish influence cannot only be seen and appreciated, it can be experienced. It has a pulse of its own that serves as a basis for a more complete understanding of one of the most significant periods in history — a time for the flourishing of the Arabic culture; a place for the expression of singularly unique art forms.

The Alhambra is living proof of the enduring influence of the Moors and the Arabic influence throughout Western Europe. It is testimony to the hundreds of years of tradition and cultural development that is rooted not only in Spain, but in Greece, Yugoslavia, Austria, and most of the land surrounding the Mediterranean and Black Sea.

Patterns and motifs carved into its stone, wood, and metalworks have been copied by generations of crocheters, lace-makers, weavers, knitters, and other artisans many years before pattern books were even conceived, much less published.

During the sweep of history that represents this vast area known as the Ottoman Empire, it was a fundamental belief that everyone should develop mastery at some trade or occupation. Recognized crafts were woodcarving, silversmithing, metal inlaying, gem setting, weaving, and the other textile hand works.

From generation to generation, Persians and Arabs established a discipline in design that is simple, yet complex; geometric, yet flowing; formalized, yet delicate; commanding, yet subtle.

The entire Mediterranean Region was constantly invaded and occupied by a mixture of cultures which has added special and unique flavors to all of the arts. An example of this cultural blending is evident in the design motifs on the Cathedral in Sevilla, Spain. The cathedral itself is a combination of segments that were built by the 6th Century Visigoths, to the 12th Century Moors, to the 17th Century Christians. The special mixed motif is called "Mudejar" and combines the Christian and Moorish design in one motif. It is also known as "sebka" and "ataurique."

Another example of this cultural mixing of design can be found on the other side of Europe, in Zagreb, Yugoslavia. St. Mark's Church displays many design patterns that were popular from the 12th through the 19th Centuries. Here, designs were created and adapted to reflect changing influences of the various nations which ruled the area from time to time across generations.

This mixture of cultural influence is typical of other such architectural structures. During major reconstruction in 1880, the sculptor Mihanovic carved a popular rose motif into the portal of the Zagreb Cathedral. Mysteriously, this motif was known in other parts of the world as the famous "Irish Rose" featured in Irish Crochet. These rose motifs are identical. They were produced at the same time in many distant lands and cultures.

Also, special church articles played a central role in ideas for crochet design. Nuns often copied designs from ornate altar chalices which often featured floral motifs, geometric designs, or designs of religious symbolism that date back to antiquity.

Patterns found in virtually all parts of the Mediterranean, Adriatic, and Aegean regions are amazingly similar in shape, ornamentation, embellishment, delicate coloring, and technique. Separated by thousands of miles and generations of time, the continuity of both pattern and design in the handicraft arts of this vast region clearly demonstrates a common tradition or influence that has survived, and indeed prospered until modern times.

New concepts for design ideas, techniques, and various applications for crochet patterns were developing all across the Continent and in England by the 16th Century. After all, crochet derived its name from the French. It borrowed its patterns from ancient and medieval civilizations, as well as from the well-established Greek, Italian, and Spanish Point Laces.

However, it was in Ireland where crochet achieved its perfection in artistry. There, it became known simply as "Irish Crochet" during the 19th Century. This exquisite "Irish Crochet" developed in the hands of benevolent upper class ladies and Irish nuns. It was never promoted with a profit in mind beyond that which would benefit the crochet worker.

The portal of the cathedral in Zagreb, Yugoslavia

Detail of the stone rose carved into the portal of the Zagreb Cathedral during the 1800s.

The world-famous crocheted Irish Rose, mysteriously identical to the stone rose on the Zagreb Cathedral – a continent apart.

Chain laces and other needle-laces worked during the 16th through the 18th Centuries in Ireland by skilled professionals, are important to the history and art of crochet. Examples of costly vestments and mantles for the Church, heavy tapestries, trimmings, and embroideries made with threads of silver and gold, all took part in the development of crochet. Gilt edges, precious metals twisted and braided into white and yellow threads, added new dimensions to the craftsmanship of a very old set of skills and all can be traced back to at least the 10th Century in Ireland.

Chain lace was an early form of crochet. Actual references to this and other forms of crochet in Ireland are seen to have first emerged through the promotional efforts of the Dublin Society, which was later incorporated and renamed the Royal Dublin Society by the year 1749.

It was an organization established and dedicated to the social and economic progress of Ireland. It provided grants of money to encourage and aid "improvements of all kinds ... to measure, understand, and express progress in the arts with appropriate incentives...."

The Society also helped to promote and publicize the needlecrafts. At this time in history, the urge to imitate Venetian Lace and other world famous lace points became the dedication of thousands — men, women, and children. Setting a standard of excellence for technique, developing skills, and finding new markets for the collective work products soon became major new activities of the Society.

Beginning its major work in 1731, it became an important benefactor for artisans throughout the country. By 1743, money was awarded to the children of workhouses to further encourage the production of Bone Lace. The records show that in 1755, a prize of two pounds was awarded to Miss Mary Gibson for her "Cheyne Lace" piece. Ironically by that time, "cheyne" lace was an art that had been relatively unheard of since the 16th Century days of Queen Elizabeth I.

A name of monumental importance to the development and nurturing of Irish Crochet Lace as a means of economic self-sufficiency for thousands of Irish men, women, and children, is that of Honoria (Nano) Nagle. Throughout her sixty-six-year life, she dedicated her considerable energies to helping the poor — to teaching them the crafts of needlework.

She was born in Ballygriffin in 1718, and grew up in Ireland during a time when suppression and bigotry were extreme. When Nano reached the age of fourteen, her parents sent her to Paris for more schooling and to "make her a lady." She grew to love Paris — the excitement, fashions, the carefree hours, and all of the privileges common to aristocratic socialites of the era. Unlike many other wealthy young women, however, Nano soon learned about the plight of the poor people of Paris. She was haunted by their misery and abject poverty. The stark and bitter contrast between the lives of those poor people and her own life of privilege burned in her mind for years.

Returning to Ireland, Nano gained the support of her family and quietly began starting and operating schools for young children. She taught them manners, reading, knitting, and "the

Lace school at Presentation Convent in Youghal, County Cork, Ireland.

skills of hand that would permit them to earn a living." She soon opened seven schools that worked with some four hundred children.

Meeting the ever-increasing demands of the poverty around her, and to ensure the safety and continuation of the schools she had started for the poor, Nano dedicated years of her life to convincing the Ursuline Order to establish a convent in Ireland. Nano, along with four volunteers taking religious training in Paris, successfully opened the home of St. Angela Merci in 1771. While she supplied this convent building for the Sisters, she never lived in it. The convent was operated under her guiding hand, and became widely known for its ability to deliver a quality education and to teach the basic skills necessary for a productive life. Her school also offered the "finishing" skills associated with other convent schools of the time.

Soon, more teachers were brought to her school from France. It prospered. Legend among the old lace-makers credit Nano Nagle with bringing the art of crochet from her convent school in Paris into her new schools in Ireland. She already knew that the needlecraft art could help her students earn a living, and that crochet was a relatively easy technique to learn. She knew that traditional needlelaces were complicated and of-

ten took years to learn, whereas crochet could be learned in a few weeks using a few simple stitches.

Nano wanted to expand beyond the Ursuline system and began a new religious community that would be solely dedicated to helping all the people of Ireland who were living in poverty. So, in 1775, the Sisters of Charitable Instruction of the Sacred Heart of Jesus (later known as the Presentation Sisters) celebrated its opening in the company of fifty beggars to whom Nano, herself, served the welcoming dinner.

After Nano's death in 1784, the Ursuline and Presentation Sisters of Ireland continued their dedication to education and spiritual development. Needlework was an important part of the curriculum, and was considered a social refinement; a "skill of domestic contentment."

Steadily, the convents attracted more and more students, particularly in the southern regions of Ireland such as County Cork. Shortly after 1822, the Ursuline Convent purchased some property for a new convent in Blackrock.

Irish crochet hooks made from sawed-off sewing needles in the early days of the Irish Crochet Industry. Then, the needles were pushed into a home-made handle usually of cork or tree bark.

It was here, in the Blackrock Convent, that Irish Point Lace and a wide variety of crochet laces began their roads to perfection. From the turn of the 19th Century until at least the 1850s, it was the Ursulines who developed and capitalized upon new opportunities for needle lace workers, and their beautiful pieces.

In 1845, the Ursuline Convent in Blackrock received ninety pounds for a single piece of crochet which was made by the poor children of the school.

Such fees were often the equivalent of several months work at other trades — if employment could be found at all. Since even small children could learn to crochet, quite literally thousands of families recognized that this art could provide them with a means to survive.

The simple crochet hook was largely responsible for a nation's economic survival, and the financial well-being of individual families. The crochet hook — an unpretentious instrument — was often created at home by the Irish. They would simply cut away the "eye" portion of a common needle. This would leave a needle with a hook. Then, to create handles for their "homemade" crochet hooks, the improvised needles would be lodged securely into the center of a cork, or piece of bark from a tree.

Following the example of the Ursulines, another school was started in County Cork by J.F. Maguire that led to the creation of crochet as a full-fledged village industry. It was operated by Lady Deane of Dundanion Castle, and employed many crochet workers. Taking commissions from wealthy aristocrats in England, France, and many other countries of Western Europe, her Irish Crochet Lace became increasingly important. It was a distinct type of lace that gained favor throughout the world.

Gracehill and a number of national primary schools also trained and provided workers for the increasing crochet lace industry in Ireland. The Carmelite Convent at New Rose, in County Wexford, brought crochet to a certain perfection in style and technique — a perfection for which they became very well-known.

The growth of the industry spread outward from the crochet centers within a very short time. In fact, soon the art of crochet became included in the educational system of almost every convent in the land. The popularity of the beauti-

Two photographs of lace classes at Presentation Convent in Youghal, County Cork.

ful crochet laces created in the convents continued to grow.

Working conditions in the convent schools of Ireland during this period were austere to say the least. Workers spent long hours each day in disciplined activity that spanned from twelve to fifteen hours at a stretch.

Eventually, the Presentation Convent encouraged its workers to form a cooperative so that their work could be completely self-supporting. The teaching nuns served on a Board of Management for the new cooperative, and the Convent agreed to allow workers to use its lace-making rooms. As a cooperative enterprise, the workers could gradually be separated from dependence upon anyone except themselves and then be free to continue their lives.

Antique Irish Crochet Lace Dresses worked at the Presentation Convent in Youghal, County Cork, Ireland at the turn of the Century.

With professional instruction in crochet lace, a new and distinctive style was soon developed and refined. Quickly, the skills of crochet spread to all corners of Ireland, and were becoming increasingly popular among the masses. Work produced in Irish Crochet was exported with great success. Eager markets found that it was more durable than the finer laces. It could be easily washed and maintained without loss to its original beauty. And, perhaps most importantly, Irish Crochet was comparatively inexpensive. A full crocheted gown cost "a mere trifle" of what the same gown created in the traditional needlelace technique would have cost. The Presentation Sisters also continued to prosper in Youghal and other communities beyond Cork. They provided the basics of Catholic education and training while expanding their ministry to the poor. They continually refined their developing production of Irish Crochet Lace along with other needle laces. By the mid-1800s, there were over 12,000 crochet workers in County Cork alone. Many of these were very poor and looked to crochet and their benefactors at convent schools to show them hope for a brighter future, and command the skills for a new beginning.

The Royal Dublin Society began its patronage of crochet because the art was quickly adaptable to the needs and wants of everyday living. Little skill was necessary for its execution when compared to the laces that were commonplace at the time.

Further, the records of the Society are replete with references to the fact that crochet materials cost far less than the more expensive and finer threads used for lace-making. One of their publications announced that "...the peasantry along with our children can quickly learn this art and reap the rewards there from..."

Most recognized, promoted, and developed within the Irish crochet styles are those known as "Irish Point," "Raised Rose," and "Honiton Point." The latter was named for the well-known Honiton Laces of Nottingham and other communities in England.

There were many characteristics from the older needle lace styles which were adapted and designed into "Irish Crochet." The delicate fineness or intricacy was made possible by the crochet stitches imitating the simple buttonhole stitch, a staple for most needle-made laces. Irish workers developed crochet into a new artform that became known as "Irish Crochet Lace."

Many thousands of families in Ireland were to learn and practice the new art of Irish Crochet Lace. They learned its techniques, mastered its skills, and were able to take full advantage of the art as their sole means of economic survival. Their new skills in the crochet arts brought thousands of poor people of Ireland through major food shortages and famines that crippled their country economically for more than twenty years. Individual families were able to make and sell beautiful pieces of crochet — a special kind of beauty that was born of pain and desperation. Crocheters did not starve. Consistent with its initial Charter, the Royal Dublin Society promoted crochet and all the needlecraft arts of Ireland not only at home, but throughout England, Western Europe, Colonial America, and the West Indies.

The importance of the contributions made by the Presentation and other convents of Southern Ireland, as well as the Royal Dublin Society itself during the early part of the 19th Century, must be set in a proper context for understanding.

Ireland had experienced widespread crop failures on many occasions, but none so severe as their "potato famines" of the 1840s and '50s. Infected with a fungal disease which caused their potatoes to rot as they grew, these major famines claimed the lives of more than a million Irish people in less than a decade.

Western sections of Ireland that were least able to cope with the disaster were hardest hit. Compounding their agricultural problems were the coldest and wettest of winters, followed by yet more potato crop failures. Each successive year of failure drove farm workers into the depths of a great depression. Across the rolling hills of Ireland

Interior of a cabin depicting the poverty in the West and South of Ireland. Courtesy of the Bettman Archive.

and down to the edge of the sea, people huddled in dark cabins. Children were covered with rags and sat together in smoke-filled rooms by their open hearths on the verge of death. In the cities, there were whispers of old people begging for help. Tenements were overcrowded. Suffering continued year after year with the common plea, "Tha shein uchrais!" (I am hungry!).

Unable to pay their rent, many of the Irish poor were evicted. Some villages were burned to the ground. Poor people died in the streets from starvation.

Wealthy and absentee landowners found it more profitable to grow cattle for export to England than to raise alternative crops for food at home. Cattle, hogs, and grain were shipped out of all major ports in Ireland as a means of commercial profit, while the poor looked on and realized a dwindling number of options for survival.

In some ninety-two separate districts of Ireland, workhouses were established by the government to provide meager assistance through the Poor Law Unions. Here at least, local destitutes were able to find some food and shelter. It is recorded that some administrators of these workhouses considered poverty a disease rather than as an economic reality. As a result, most workhouses were miserable places. They had little heat, porridge, and perhaps only a bowl of soup. Families were separated. Diseases spread. Little medical attention was available, and for the most part, the people could not pay for it even when it was.

Government relief programs were ineffective, and often became administrative nightmares. English political leaders clung to a "hands-off" policy, and did little to help alleviate the crisis in Ireland. Thousands of people emigrated in what became known as "coffin ships," because so many of them were so weak and sick that they died at sea. Out of this was born one of the most beautiful forms of crochet the world has ever known.

Often using homemade hooks and inexpensive cotton threads, crochet workers in a network of cooperatives became known as "flower-

The Irish Famine – at the gate of the Work House. Courtesy of the Bettman Archive.

ers," "spriggers," or "parcellers." For them, crochet was a blessed opportunity to compete, to enjoy the company of friends, and to use their skills as a source of cash. Weekly payments to young girls working in a cooperative during the 1850s was perhaps six to fifteen shillings a week. After the tragedies of the famine, workers found they could earn more from crochet than from specialty laces.

Where embroideries on net using darned or chain stitches was a painstaking effort requiring perhaps weeks to produce a single motif, crochet appliques could be turned out in a few hours. When cambric or linen work to produce classic guipure styles might take months, its imitation in crochet could be produced four times faster.

Through crochet, poor women and children could survive. They could produce an income and gain respectability through the work of their own hands. People began to identify crochet as "Nun's Lace" or "Poor Man's Lace."

Another important figure in the development of Irish Crochet Lace was Mrs. Susannah Meredith. Her "Adelaide Industrial School," founded in 1847, was to become famous not only in Ireland, but throughout England and France. She did much to maintain high quality standards from her workers, as well as develop a constant supply of new patterns, stitches, and techniques.

Mrs. Meredith was also of singular importance to the crochet industry in Ireland because commercial success was also one of her ambitions. At its peak, her Adelaide School paid well over one hundred pounds a week to the most skilled workers. One child, for example, earned enough to rescue her mother and sisters from their life in a workhouse. Later, they also became crochet workers learning the techniques of the "best selling" Adelaide House.

In a dingy, backstreet building that also served as a depot for relief services, a typical crochet class of 1848 was taught to as many as one hundred and forty people at a time. Children, often grimy and sick, were eager to attend the cooperative school because food would be served. A teacher presided over the group and showed them how to divide a ball of thread and use hooks to make crochet edgings. Sometimes, a buyer would come to the school and take the finished pieces to an agent who could sell them in England and elsewhere.

Alice Smyth of Monaghan, an Irish Crochet expert, 1870. Private collection, Eithne D'Arcy.

Sometimes called "Relief Lace," the art of Irish Crochet Lace continued in its refinement and sophistication. Its appeal spread. A people survived.

Even men of the villages and outlying farms came to the schools to learn. Many of them were already too weak and too starved to do a job that was considered hard labor; crochet was an easier way of life. The quality of their work was often inconsistent, and it became a very real problem for the schools to turn out a smooth, finished piece from all of the varied sections made by different people at different times.

Women were in a hurry to make and sell their crochet. Often, their workmanship also suffered. Sometimes, they completed their work without regard to the patterns before them and resented correction or direction from their teachers. According to the records kept by Mrs. Meredith, some of the workers became "...bored with this same shamrock pattern that is ordered for a mere 5 shillings when the pine patterned work is more interesting to do."

One worker commented: "...I like crochet best, ma'am, because there's hope in it. I may get ever so much for what I make, if I happen to hit on a new stitch, and all the time I'm at it, I don't know but I may have a lot of money coming to me, and I'm keep in spirits like, to the last moment..."

"The Lacemakers," 1865.

The idea for cooperative schools as primary school training in needlework arts penetrated the northern regions of Ireland by the 1850s.

Mrs. W.C. Roberts of Thorton, Kildare, for example, attracted workers in large numbers to her school. All members of families participated and within the space of ten years, she placed twenty-eight of her trained crochet teachers in as many distressed areas throughout Ireland.

One of Mrs. Robert's teachers was received at a rectory in Clones, the center of a poor mountainous district. The Reverend Thomas Hand and his wife, Cassandra, used crochet as the means through which the people of the region could survive. Under the tutelage and support of Mrs. Roberts, her teacher, and the Hands, men and women of the Clones area eagerly learned new designs, bars, and stitches that quickly brought

Crochet workers in Ireland. Courtesy of the Presentation Convent, Youghal, County Cork, Ireland.

Clones Crochet to the market where it commanded good prices. Typical of the Clones style were motifs of roses, daisies, shamrocks, ferns, vines, and grape patterns along with wild flowers and insects common to the Irish countryside.

shipped to churches, rectories, cooperatives, and other points of distribution for waiting world markets.

Cassandra Hand had a shrewd sense of marketing. She encouraged new designs and began

Glass globe filled with water to reflect the light from a nearby lamp, enabling the crochet workers to continue long after dark. Private Collection, Annie Potter.

Worked between farm chores and often outdoors to take full advantage of sunlight, the new skills of crochet were practiced, developed and sold. After dark, work could only be accomplished by the light of a slow-burning peat fire, or an old lamp with a reflecting glass globe of water.

Within two short years, there were some 1,500 workers employed in "Parish Crochet" as a result of the efforts of Reverend Hand and his wife. Some was made in homes that were dingy, dirty, and poverty-stricken with muddy surroundings. To make any work saleable, it first had to be thoroughly washed.

Fortunately, crochet pieces are easy to wash and are far more sturdy than most conventional laces. Once washed, the original brilliance of white or ivory cotton thread would return. Carefully packed, consignment pieces were then

to specialize in crochet that was different from work then being produced in Southern Ireland. She developed a style based on the Church lace from old Spanish monasteries and convents which became known as "Jesuit Crochet" and "Spanish Crochet."

The crocheted Clones knot developed in Clones, Ireland. Private collection, Eithne D'Arcy.

The Clones District was also known for a type of crochet known as "Guipure." Here, a plain style and simple variety was formed of closely arranged crochet stitching and bars.

More complicated versions of the technique included what is now recognized in the world of crochet as the "Clones Knot."

Raised, lifted above a background network or pattern, tightly-wound Clones Knots added dimension and interest to spaces between other designs and motifs.

The idea quickly caught fire and spread throughout the crochet industry as a new variation to design.

Lifted crochet guipure also became a new fashion treatment for dresses, blouses, cuffs, collars, edgings, and jabots of lace.

Irish Crochet Lace could replace the beauty of traditional lace points at a much lower cost.

Crochet Lace was now affordable for millions of people in rising middle-class markets who wanted to imitate some of the costly laces still being worn by the very rich, the elite in society, and even royalty.

Through the organization and leadership of the Irish Cooperatives, other societies and technical institutions developed to encourage the growing crochet industry.

On solid footing, the Irish Agricultural Technical Institution and the Cookstown Home Industries Society, for example, refined assembly line methods of production that were efficient and profitable during this period.

Some workers specialized in new designs. Others devoted themselves to crocheting motifs, or sprigs, as they were called. Still others would sew motifs in patterns on paper backings.

More would fill in grounds with connecting bars and picots. Finally, still more workers would do headings and edgings.

Together, they could turn out their consignment pieces and orders more quickly and all were able to earn more money faster.

Antique Irish Sprigs, the beginning step in creating Irish Crochet Lace.

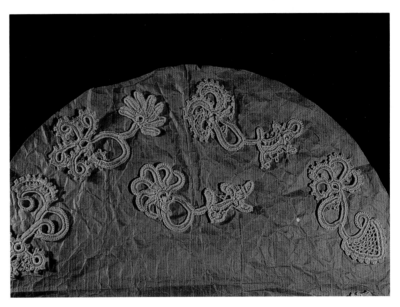

Finished Sprigs were arranged and sewn to a paper backing.

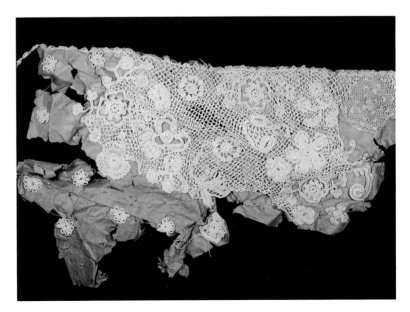

Fill-in crochet was worked around the motifs. Later, the paper backing was cut away.

Crochet became so successful as a new industry in Ireland that it was featured in the Dublin Exhibition of 1853. Crochet was finally recognized as the native art that was the pride of a nation. Exciting. Affordable. Profitable.

Few designers were available during these years of rapid growth, however, to create new patterns, assortments of fresh motifs, and mixtures of new styles for crochet laces. Design and quality were sometimes sacrificed for speed of production.

The Countess of Aberdeen was also very important to the spread of crochet as an artform. She, like Mlle. Riego, believed that good and suitable design was of critical importance to the Irish Lace industry. Lady Aberdeen reflected that, "The ultimate object should be to make each piece of lace a work of art, like a picture, the design of which is not to be repeated, but to be cherished by its owner as a valuable possession."

Mlle. Riego later commented, "Being a lover of all artistic lace, I quite agree with the good Countess, for it was in this spirit that the beautiful Lace of the past was produced, and could be again if met with sufficient encouragement.... for the Irish workers possess talent if properly directed..... bear in mind that works of art cannot be accomplished if price is very limited, and that formerly, in the demand for cheapness, good work and design were often overlooked."

Lady Aberdeen, wife of Lord Haddo, was a woman of incredible energy and charity. She was a friend to every Dublin almshouse and hospital — visiting regularly, tending to the spirit and well-being of the sick and the poor.

Educated in London and a native of Scotland, Lady Aberdeen raised five children and was, for many years, active in the social scene of London. She and her family moved to Ireland after her husband was appointed Viceroy. There, she did considerable work for the "betterment of the communities," including organizing an Exhibition of Irish Home Industries and planning for the "Mansion House Ladies' Committee for the Relief of the Distress."

On her many tours through the lacemaking centers of Ireland, she established a good relationship with the nuns of the convents and poor workers of the villages and towns. She came to understand the need to improve the marketing of Irish lace and crochet products. As a direct result of seeing this need first-hand, she purchased the Lace Depot at 76 Grafton Street that would serve as a sales distribution outlet for Irish needlecrafts.

Committed to doing all she could to help the Irish people make a living through their arts, she was instrumental in organizing an "Irish Goods" exhibit in the Irish Village at the Chicago World's Fair in 1893. Thanks in large measure to this important exposure across the Atlantic, Irish Crochet lace became recognized and appreciated in the Americas and throughout Western Europe.

The tireless energies of people such as Lady Aberdeen and Mlle. Riego, along with their marketing genius and resources, were coupled with an increasing number of pattern book publishers that emerged during this same time period. The art of crochet reached its peak of world favor during the latter part of the 19th Century — a crest of popularity that was to continue for follow-

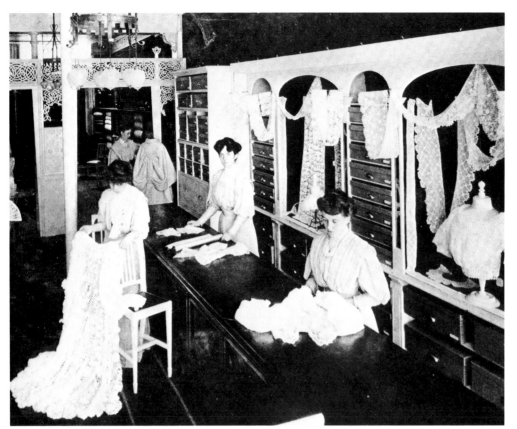

Lace Depot at 76 Grafton Street that served as a distribution outlet for the Irish Needlecrafts. Courtesy of Michael O'Connell, Pro Media.

Some 300,000 women were employed in sewing or muslin work, principally in the Southern regions of Ireland at the beginning of the 19th Century. It is estimated that another 20,000 people were working as lace-makers. Such a work force provided desperately needed income and enjoyed a mortal blessing of having something important to do that would fill long hours of each working day.

Within a short time, Irish Crochet, made by the poor workers, was providing new fashions in crochet that were in great demand throughout Paris, London, Vienna, and Brussels — to name but a few of their expanding market areas.

An example of the widespread popularity of Irish Crochet is an exquisite dress made for a Spanish noblewoman, Sr. Anna Vidal de Rocamora. It was made for her in 1910 and is perfectly preserved by the Museo Textil y de Indumentaria in Barcelona. It is a beautiful example of the three-dimensional approach to Irish crochet, and it has hundreds of individual motifs in an astonishing variety that are placed onto the gown in swirls of patterns for a

ing generations and firmly establish crochet as an important "Lady's Art" among the needlecrafts.

Through the 1800s, the Irish crochet and lace-makers continued their work, developing, refining, and marketing thousands of finished pieces. A variety of Irish laces were well-known to the world markets, and the lace trade provided a source of income for thousands of skilled workers, even during the long years of famine.

The work of most Irish lace-makers was done with the support and encouragement of the Royal Dublin Society. By stimulating the national activity in lace-making, as well as in the art of crochet, the Society devoted its energies to the development of all needlework arts.

The Society, convent schools, regular crochet schools, and early co-operatives recognized that markets were ripe for a lace that would be easily and quickly learned. Even children could help develop crochet into the much needed, well-paying industry.

Irish Crocheted Collars and Cuffs produced in the Presentation Convent in Youghal, County Cork Ireland.

Irish Crocheted Collar produced in the Presentation Convent in Youghal, County Cork, Ireland.

layered effect. Truly a fine example of the description of Irish Crochet is that it is carved ivory in lace.

Besides working crochet, the workers were also adapting other lace-making techniques such as the flat and raised needlepoint, applique lace, and drawn work in the style of Italian cut points and Reticella. A story about the importance of the crochet and lace industry in Ireland would not be complete without some mention of a few of these other laces.

For example, in the mid-1800s, the patience of Mother Mary Ann Smyth of the Presentation Convent in Youghal, County Cork, was responsible for the development of another Irish lace. A "very fine and exquisite piece of antique Italian Lace" came into her possession. For weeks, she studied it and attempted to make a pattern from it that she and others might follow and duplicate. Finally, unravelling it — thread by thread, stitch by stitch — she was able to learn the techniques that were used in the creation of the piece. She then taught her brightest students how to copy the stitches.

Soon, she was able to establish another lace-making school in 1852 that produced the distinctive "Youghal Lace." This form was made with a sewing needle, a single, continuous thread, and a buttonhole-stitching technique. Youghal

Lace was gradually improved and developed to such an extent that this particular Irish point was soon singled out and established as a native Irish Art.

The technique continued to spread and within a few short years, was taught in other convent schools throughout the region — areas such as Kenmare, Killarney, New Ross, and even in some of the Church of Ireland schools in the North.

For well over fifty years, the Presentation Convent at Youghal continued to build its traditions as a lace center without any outside financial support. All of the profits went directly to the workers. Crochet lace was taught and made side by side with the famous Youghal needlepoint lace.

Also, new technological developments in England during the 1800s meant that other new laces could be developed. John Heathcote's inven-

Antique Irish Crochet Collar worked in the late 1800s. Private Collection, Eithne D'Arcy.

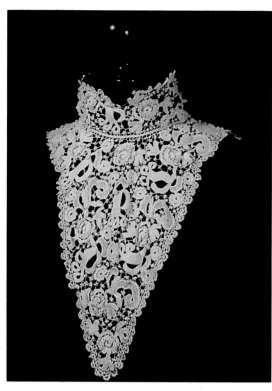

Antique Irish Crochet Collar worked in the late 1800s. Private Collection, Eithne D'Arcy.

tion of machinemade cotton net in 1809 was one such advancement.

Embroideries of machinemade net provided a "look of lace" that closely matched older and more expensive pieces, and they could be produced for a fraction of the cost and time.

Irish laces that resulted from machinemade net became known as Carrickmacross, in the year 1820; Kells, in 1825; and Limerick, in 1829.

Modern historian Ms. Nellie O'Cleirigh, in her sensitive account of Irish traditions in lace-making titled "Carrickmacross Lace: Irish Embroidered Net Lace," has provided excellent documentation for the role played by the lace industries in her native Ireland. An expert in the field, she has personally known life in the Ursuline Convent Schools, as well as in the University College of Dublin. A collector and exhibitor of old Irish lace and embroideries, Ms. O'Cleirigh has become a recognized authority on the history of both Limerick and Carrickmacross laces.

Her detailed account of lace-making in Ireland during the 18th and 19th Centuries concludes that "... the great era of Irish, as of European lace-making, ended with the outbreak of World War I in 1914 .... although today there is yet another revival of interest in both Limerick and Carrickmacross laces of a high standard." An art, to be worthy of the name, will survive. Beauty cannot be denied. A love for excellence can never be forgotten.

To help ensure that fact, in a small cottage just inside the border of Northern Ireland, Eithne D'Arcy still carries on the traditions of lace-making and Irish Crochet Lace. As a specialist, author,

and designer, both crochet and lace have been a daily part of her life since early childhood.

Specializing in the styles of crochet that flourished in Fermanagh and Monaghan Counties of Ireland, Mrs. D'Arcy has dedicated her retirement years to documenting and preserving Irish history as it was experienced through the lace arts.

She has an extensive collection of lace and crochet that has been carefully nurtured over the years. She inherited some of it from long-established friends and family who freely gave her their most treasured pieces in their wills. Other pieces have come to her as gifts — to recognize Mrs. D'Arcy's work on behalf of a shared profession.

Eithne D'Arcy, a soft-spoken, internationally-loved spokeswoman of Irish Crochet, has documented the lives of earlier lace-makers with intimate stories, sincere warmth, and a captivating spirit. To her, crochet is a way of life. It is a language of beauty that an artist uses to transform a simple ball of thread into lasting pieces of art.

Modern Ireland, as well as those days of national crisis a hundred years ago, can be experienced in the crochet work that has now become a symbol of life, hope, and pride. Here, Mrs. D'Arcy — herself, the essence of "Erin" (Ireland) — is determined that the human spirit of Irish history will continue to be

Identical Irish Crochet Motifs. The smaller motif was worked with the fine thread of the 1800s. The larger motif was worked with thread that is considered "fine" by today's standards. Private Collection, Eithne D'Arcy.

revealed through the legacy of the famous Irish lace arts which are known and respected throughout the world.

The Irish shamrocks, wild flowers, and roses — along with the Clones knot, half scroll, and motifs unique to particular regions of Ireland

Irish Crochet dress worn by Anna Vidal I Sola de Rocamora at the turn of the Century. Courtesy of the Museo Textil y de Indumentaria, Spain. **119**

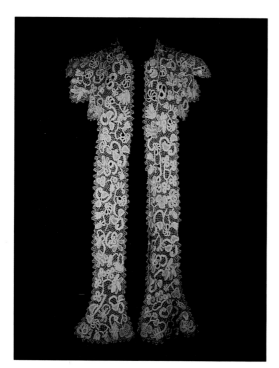

Antique Irish Crochet Collar worn during the turn of the Century. Private Collection, Annie Potter.

Antique Irish Crochet Collar from the turn of the Century. Private Collection, Annie Potter.

— and especially the simple beauty of a splendid people are expressed in Irish Crochet Lace.

As an industry, Irish Crochet Lace began to flatten out in the mid-1860s. There was a brief revival of Irish Crochet Lace during the 1870s. Continental laces were harder to obtain because of the Franco-Prussian War. Then, the industry once again faltered.

About ten years later, the Irish Crochet Lace industry was marked by unscrupulous merchants, the abuse of art in favor of profits alone, and the introduction of machinemade embroideries and laces. As a result of at least these three factors, Irish crochet workers by the thousands lost their enthusiasm for the craft.

Another reason that this most exquisite "Irish Crochet" faltered, was that it developed in the hands of the benevolent upper class ladies and the Irish nuns, and it was never promoted with a profit in mind beyond that of the crochet worker. Their skills fell into lethargy. Demand for hand made crochet pieces fell sharply. Markets dried up. Interests shifted to the mass production of cheaper, although inferior pieces. Expert design gave way to repetition of what would sell best. Quality became subservient to quantity.

A letter from Mrs. W.C. Roberts to Mrs. Meredith, two of Ireland's best known teachers of Irish Crochet Lace, sadly commented that "...it will give me great pleasure to give you any information in my power respecting the crochet trade in times past; but I regret to say, it cannot at present be said to exist in these parts."

The slump that hit Irish Crochet Laces in the late 1800s was most noticeable at the Mansion House Exhibition in London during the Spring of 1883. Youghal laces were judged to be the finest and most artistic of any displayed.

The headmaster of the Cork School of Art, James Brenan, was frustrated by all the unfavorable reports that he heard about Irish Crochet at the Mansion House Exhibition. Where once laces from his part of Ireland had taken all the top honors, they now received only passing glances and courteous mention in the reviews.

Meeting with Alan S. Cole, who was also an art teacher and personal friend, the two decided to do something about what they described as a "most sad state of affairs to find our native crafts in such disrepair." Together, they raised the sum of 500 pounds that would be given as a prize for the best and most creative new design in Irish Crochet Lace during the coming year.

They toured lace schools throughout Southern Ireland to spread the word of their prize, gathered new ideas, and made up plans for judging fresh drawings and designs. With their finely-tuned creative skills and artistic flair, they showed crochet teachers how to see the world through the eye of an artist; to see the delicate plants and flowers that bordered the green meadows, to look in new ways upon the graceful swan, a seashell, and the flowing lines of pottery. They taught groups of the best teachers they met how to understand a whole new set of possibilities that were inherent to the materials they were using. They taught them how to make crochet patterns from photographs of the old traditional laces that had made Ireland famous.

As a team, Brenan and Cole gave their new mission their total energies, and they found new ways to stimulate the old art that they both

Irish Crochet Coat from a San Francisco estate at the turn of the Century. Private Collection, Annie Potter.

loved. Thanks to their efforts, they could see through the eyes of new artists once again.

James Brenan described the crochet of the 1860s as "a deterioration of style and substance sad to behold when compared to the proud traditions once held." He watched as crochet workers "...took large sheets of brown paper and cut them to the size of a desired trim or piece. Then, they scattered crochet motifs over the paper in a random fashion and finally hooked them together with an imitation stitch of the ties or bars from Rose Point without any special arrangement or composition..."

Seeing a new potential in what these crochet workers were doing led him to teach them a sense of composition. They learned to refine their process of arranging motifs for artistic balance, to direct the flowing lines of raised patterns, and to help workers experience a new freedom of design that led directly to what would become

the most famous of all Irish laces, the beautiful "Irish Point."

Through the efforts of Brenan and Cole, a new system of teacher certification was set into place that recognized superior skills of workers who mastered their new techniques. Certified teachers earned larger salaries and were also interested in selling their products as "the very best available from Ireland." Among those recognized as masters of the new craft of Irish Point were Mrs. M. Lynam from Enniskillen, who offered summer courses for other crochet teachers working in her part of the country. Sister M. Columba, another certified crochet teacher and innovator from the Convent of Mercy at Wexford, taught in the cooperative industry that was run by her convent. Working with the same basic techniques, these two designers made crochet pieces of every conceivable kind and exported their work to England, France, Austria, Canada, and the United States. Through their work and promotion of "Irish Point" and "Irish Crochet Lace," they led the way for hundreds of others who felt a new excitement in the rediscovery of crochet as a handicraft art.

The Irish Industries Association and the Department of Agricultural and Technical Instruction, along with the Lace Depot, began to hunt for new marketing channels and the Con-

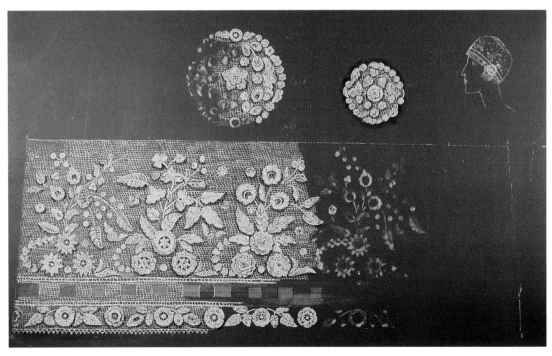

An artist's pattern board used to guide a crochet worker in Ireland.

Detail of machine-made Irish crochet. Private Collection, Annie Potter.

gested Districts Board was also helpful in trying to stabilize the Irish crochet industry.

Stimulated by their new success and the prices that their Irish Point commanded on the world markets, new heights of activity were set into motion. Teachers took their new skills to students in cities throughout the country, as well as to the rural schools and cooperatives to enlist ever-increasing numbers of workers to the production of Irish Point and Irish Crochet Laces.

One of the most famous post-famine crochet schools was started by Lady Gore-Booth in a room of a square of buildings in the woods of County Sligo. Taught by Miss Elizabeth Flanagan, the women produced collars, table linens, christening gowns, and other pieces that were marketed by Lady Gore-Booth, and which later became a thriving cooperative business.

In good weather, workers preferred to work outside. Under a shade tree, beside a stream or pond, or sitting on a rocky outcropping overlooking the sea, women and children made their crochet from designs they found around them. An interesting flower, stem arrangement, bush, or bird would catch their eye and they would experiment with ways to capture these ideas directly from nature and build them into their crochet pieces. Often staying outdoors until long after dark, many continued to work by the flickering light of a candle or an oil lamp.

The richness of life in the Irish countryside was once again being felt. Women and young girls perched atop a sea wall working their crochet pieces created an idyllic picture. Emerald green meadows. Grazing sheep. Stone fences and hedgerows. Thatch-covered cottages. Flowers. The lilt of a song and the laughter of children painted a picture that was to capture the hearts of the world. It represented wholesome, traditional values from a people that had renewed their spirit as well as their art.

By the turn of the 20th Century, Irish crochet once again peaked to international importance. Exhibitions worldwide helped to promote the demand for these unique crochet laces and workers reaped unprecedented benefits because they were able to earn small fortunes for their efforts. With the freedom of new techniques, even the youngest crocheters were designing their own pieces and "Point d'Irlande" was the term used for that country's most distinctive laces at this time.

The most important market for Ireland's needlecrafts was nearby England, and particularly among aristocratic women. It is said that women became addicted to their crochet needles learning from the Irish as well as from other important centers such as France, Italy, and Belgium. For example, Queen Victoria purchased some Irish-made thread socks for her young prince and princesses and decked them out with collars, scarves, gloves, dresses, and all manner of crochet pieces that they proudly wore at state ceremonies and other important events.

Most of Ireland, with the exception of the industries in the North, was little affected by the

Irish Crochet dress in a shop window. Courtesy of the Presentation Convent, Youghal, County Cork Ireland.

Two-piece afternoon dress of Irish Crochet Lace in floral pattern from 1905. New York Metropolitan Museum.

in their small, uncomfortable berths.

An 1847 traveler who made the trip in the steerage section wrote: "...Before the emigrant has been a week at sea, he is an altered man. How could it be otherwise? Hundreds of poor people, men, women, and children of all ages, from the driveling idiot of ninety to the babe just born, huddled together without air, wallowing in filth, and breathing a fetid atmosphere, sick in body and dispirited in heart."

Almost two million Irish emigrated to the United States between 1845 and 1859. By the year 1900, that number grew to four million.

After arrival, they held onto their strong Irish traditions, and even though the new arrivals were considered poor by American standards, they were considered rich by Irish standards. For example, a former Adelaide School student wrote home from America saying that she could now afford to dress better than many of her former patrons.

A group of young Irish girls passed the window of a large New York department store, Bloomingdale's, and seeing a crochet dress in the window were able to identify the women who had worked on the assembly of the dress and who made the motifs. Techniques and the levels of skill going into the making of crochet pieces were as recognizable to them as the signatures of the workers might have been.

Industrial Revolution. The country was sorely lacking in coal, iron, and people trained with the special skills required to develop major industries. After the massive crop failures, the people of Ireland often worked their crochet for passage money as well as for survival.

Over a million Irish people emigrated during the Great Famine and continued to do so in the post-famine era. In fact, emigration became an Irish tradition and that process became a major factor in Ireland's sociological makeup. The growth of the Irish community in America was to become an Irish political issue.

Irish people left their native land in crowded immigrant boats surrounded by disease and filth. They hoped to survive for the promise of a new beginning "in the green fields of America."

The majority traveled to America on sailing ships often taking four to ten weeks to arrive. The quality of the vessels ranged from passenger ships to timber cargo vessels and all were at the mercy of the wind and rough seas.

The immigrants were most often in the steerage section of these ships. They ate and slept

Even after the Irish immigrants first arrived in America, they remained more Irish than American in their ways and continued to relate to the problems of their native country for many years. The crochet lace techniques that they brought with them from England and Ireland were adapted and gradually evolved into a creation that was to become uniquely American in flavor and design.

In her 1854 publication of the "Ladies Complete Guide to Crochet, Fancy Knitting, and Needlework," Mrs. Anna S. Stephens wrote,

"In England and Ireland, where the ladies are always industrious, Crochet work has risen to the dignity of an art... In this country, crochet work can only be denominated an accomplishment, but we must consider it not merely as an elegant way of wiling away time but as one of those gentle means by which women are kept feminine and lady-like in this fast age...On no occasion does a lady seem more lovely than when half occupied with some feminine art which keeps her fingers employed, and gives an excuse for downcast eyes and gentle pre-occupation...With a crochet needle in the hand, we join more pleasantly in conversation; the little implement fills up all embarrassing pauses: its use gives a feminine and domestic air, which men may smile at, but cannot condemn; and under all circumstances, it is better than counting beads, like the modern Greeks, or flirting fans, like the Spanish belles—or flirting without fans, as sometimes happens to ladies of all nations...Every lady knows how many heart-tremors can be carried off in a vigorous twist of the crochet-needle."

It was the mid-19th Century flood of immigration that really created the early development of the crochet arts in America. Even though the Pima Indians had practiced a very primitive form of crochet many years earlier, the Colonial American women were apparently uninvolved in any form of the crochet art as it is known today. Spinning, weaving, and knitting were common activities described in the literature of the Colonial Period. There is no evidence that women like Martha Washington or Dolly Madison had even heard of crochet as a home needlecraft.

One lady described her visit with Martha Washington as: "... we thought we would visit Lady Washington, and as she was said to be so grand a lady, we thought we must put on our best bibbs and bands. So we dressed ourselves in our most elegant ruffles and silks, and were introduced to her ladyship. And don't you think we found her knitting and with a speckled (check) apron on! ....there we were without a stitch of work, and sitting in State, but General Washington's lady with her own hands knitting stockings for herself and her husband."

American women were also busy making patchwork quilts and braided rugs. Pioneer cabins required a kind of special lifestyle which was so different from the European lifestyle. The warm quilts were more important to the American pioneer family than the fancy European laces.

For those women who did carry on the old world lace-making traditions, the potential mar-

Crochet... "one of those gentle means by which women are kept feminine and lady-like in this fast age." The Crochet Worker by William Etty, mid 1800s. Courtesy of the York City Art Gallery.

ket place and distribution channels were restricted. During colonial times, George II of England enacted severe penalties for importing embroidery, brocade, and lace from the colonies. Those who brought their skill and equipment to this country were frozen out of the markets by England. The colonists believed, as one writer commented, that the English government "would burn our embroidery or lace, if we dared to send it tither."

The earliest examples of American crochet reveal an obvious Irish influence with the style of rosettes, leaves, picots and other motifs. Instruction books and pattern books became more plentiful; threadmakers also published booklets for crochet design. In 1836, "Godey's Lady's Book" was edited by Sarah Josepha Buell Hale, a New Hampshire widow with five children. It became one of the most popular pioneer magazines among American women as they settled down in late afternoon to study the latest pattern.

She also edited "Ladies' Magazine" in 1827. She wrote, "Every husband may rest assured that nothing found in these pages shall cause her (his wife) to 'usurp station' or encroach upon the prerogatives of men."

Hale then quietly crusaded for American women and their rights and was also instrumental in the establishment of Thanksgiving as a national holiday in America. Her credo was, "The home, not the public arena, was woman's battleground;

her weapons were education, conversation, delicacy, femininity, and the power to persuade; and her role was that of God's moral agent on Earth."

Looking back at Godey's in 1889, a critic termed Godey's a leading magazine of the past and wrote that it was filled with "fashion pictures, and stories supposed to be adapted by virtue of their domestic imbecility to the taste of the women of the period."

Pattern page from "Godey's Lady's Book" from the mid 1800s.

During that period, women also read and sent drawings and instructions to other magazines such as "New Idea Woman's Magazine" and "The Ladies World." In 1844, "A Winter Gift for Ladies — Instruction in Knitting, Netting, and Crochet Work" was published in New York and offered the newest and most fashionable patterns from the latest London editions, which were then revised and enlarged by an American woman.

Mrs. Pullman, a London lady who worked with the leading periodicals of the London press, published the "Ladies Manual of Fancy Work" in New York in 1858.

Other American publications of the time included: "The Ladies' Work Table" in Philadelphia during 1850, "The Ladies' Self Instructor" in 1853, and "The Ladies Guide to Needlework" by S. Annie Frost of New York in 1877.

Crochet, because of its sturdier, heavier and more practical textures, was more conducive to the American Pioneer lifestyle of the mid-1800s than was the more tra-

Crocheted bedspread from the 1950s. Courtesy of Annie's Attic.

ditional and delicate European lace. Manufacturers began producing a special cotton. With greater availability of materials as well as designs, the popularity of crochet increased and spread throughout the country.

Women enjoyed crocheting even after it was not necessary as a means of economic survival. They began to crochet as a means of making extra expense money, or simply as a relaxing activity during leisure moments, perhaps in front of a warm fire. They turned those thoughtful hours into beautiful bedspreads, table cloths, trimmings for blouses, towels, pillows, sheets; filling hope chests and baby wardrobes, or making filet cloth for drapery. Women were steadily churning out pieces with spirals, pinwheels, the star, the spider web, the pineapple and the popular popcorn stitch all with roots in ancient history, but young and exciting in new American applications.

These crocheters were also reflecting a revolutionary spirit, a freedom from tradition while clinging to an understanding of the basics, a mind-

Crocheted doily. Courtesy of Annie's Attic.

set only known in America. The women combined the symbols of many nations and added a sense of energy and freedom that was never before present in needlework. Old patterns were transformed into something that became uniquely American.

French lilies became living flowers, Dutch tulips found their way into American quilts, the English Rose became the Cherokee Rose. Soon, American motifs such as violets, daisies, and or-

chids became common elements in the crochet pieces. Filet crochet was the rage and often reflected religious symbolism by using white cotton to demonstrate purity and holiness. Women made a variety of items for the family and for the home. They used the four main stitches that led to an endless variety of stitches and form. They took advantage of an equally endless variety of yarns, ribbon, and wool. Even the invention of the sewing machine gave women more time for the fancy needlework because they could get through their plain sewing activities much more quickly.

Crochet was playing out a rhythm of its own, fingers dancing almost automatically while women watched children, visited, or relaxed and relieved boredom. One woman wrote, "It would be difficult to compute the number of hours saved by keeping a piece of knitting or crochet on hand to fill up the odd minutes, otherwise wasted, throughout the day. If a lady makes it a rule to have something of this sort at hand, ready to take up when opportunity offers, she will be amazed to discover, in a short time, how much she has accomplished."

In 1885, Laura Safford helped to initiate the Philadelphia Needlework Guild which later evolved into The Needlework Guild of America. It gave women an opportunity to meet other people, form lifelong friendships, and accomplish something worthwhile. Women made and donated garments to the Guild and then those always new, hand made clothing items were distributed among the various charitable institutions. Women and children of all ages were interested in becoming part of the venture.

Crochet became a healthy addiction, a hobby that women were excited about; they were proud of their work and began to compete with their friends to win prizes at small, local fairs. They used their own imaginations to create new designs and uses for the crochet work. It often took a life time to create a special treasure, and then it was passed down as a valuable heirloom. Even though the granny square concept originated in England,

Mollie Brown, daughter of an Irish immigrant, wearing a fashionable dress trimmed with Irish Crochet in the 19th Century. Courtesy of the Colorado Historical Society.

the granny square afghan became a tradition in American life, made with bits and pieces of leftover yarn, much like quilts made with bits of leftover material.

Granny square afghans and bedspreads have been synonymous with American crochet for generations. It was easier to do than complex crochet patterns and portable enough to do anywhere without worrying about finding a good place to stop and start on a piece. Even unrelated types of leftover yarn with a variety of color combinations could be combined to make a unique piece. The synergistic effects within the needle-work industry guided the American growth of crochet during the latter part of the 1800s and into the next century. Publications were becoming more sophisticated and increasingly available to the masses with the advancing technology in the print industry.

Competing yarn and thread companies were producing more varieties of materials and better quality products at lower prices. Good design was becoming available to the average income woman at an affordable price. Advertising and marketing techniques were generating more sales, and distribution channels for needlework products evolved not only through retail outlets, but also through direct mail sources.

Women were involved in critical positions at every level of the industry — from the operation of the thread mills, to the production of the publications, to the design stage, to the marketing and finally consumer level. Consumers were encouraged to crochet to earn extra money for themselves and their families. It was a way for women to have a sense of independence — to be separated from the "bread of dependence."

American Coke tray from the early 1900s with model dressed in Irish Crochet.

At the same time, these groups were adapting the various styles brought to America by the growing numbers of immigrants pouring into the country from all over Europe. European sources of design and technique were extremely popular such as the Maltese crochet, the hairpin work, the Russian style, the crochet imitation reticella, Battenberg, Honiton, Torchon, the Puerto Rican laces, and pieces representative of the Armenian style. Irish crochet, in particular, was one of the most popular foreign influences in American crochet. Doilies and insertions were among the most common items being crocheted, but needlewomen were also beginning to combine the other techniques, such as embroidery, with crochet in the same work. Macrame was a technique used to create certain articles that were soon more popular in the crochet form.

American crochet was reaching a peak of development, a new level of achievement and beauty during this period of extremely intense competition among the thread and yarn manufacturing companies. Outstanding pieces were created with silk, cotton, wool, and linen. The art of crochet was becoming an important factor in the American economic system. Wool producers were concentrating on products that crocheters could turn into gloves, sweaters, afghans, and shawls. Other manufacturers were trying to please the market that wanted to create fresh designs for the making of crochet lace.

Nearing the turn of the 19th Century, machinemade laces were becoming readily available and this fact largely contributed to the decline of the popularity of crochet as well as to a downturn in the development of the craft. Machinemade Irish Crochet became available in 1883. It wasn't until the late 19th Century that handmade crochet lace became fashionable again, and in the early 1900s Paris designers were showing it in their fashion collections.

Handmade crochet remained popular until the outbreak of World War I. Then, the style in America became more simple. Laces were not to be part of the new trend for easy-care clothing. Sewing machines could decorate and trim a dress very quickly. The more time-consuming process of making a hand-sewn or crocheted collar or special trimmings was also thought to give the wearer an "old-fashioned" look, or at least one that was outdated for the newer trends of the day.

The dreariness and privations known during the Great War quickly gave way to the flamboyant Roaring Twenties. At that time, legends grew up around both flappers and lounge lizards; speakeasies grew out of the Prohibition, and it was all symbolized by the sounds of freedom in a new Jazz Age. It was a rhythm that worked its way from New Orleans to the Chicago Underworld and to the college campus days of racoon-coated young men sparking with their chemise-clad entourage.

During the Great War in Europe, La Belle Epoque was ending; the "Beautiful Era" of fashionable women had been a time of blatant hypocrisy — when appearance was more important than true feelings. It was a time when the aristocracy ignored the clamor of reality which resulted in assassinations and anarchy, a time when Paris and Vienna were the fashion capitals of the world. "La Belle Epoque" was drawing to a close as predicted by a number of well-known philosophers of the times, such as Voltaire and Nietsche.

Historians point to the Great War as marking not only sweeping changes in government for people the world over, but for a revolution of mind and fashion, as well. The power and dominance of old European monarchies came to an end replaced by a new spirit and freedom for a rising middle class. Fashion turned away from the rich embroideries and lace that had marked a now rejected aristocracy and the empires they represented: titles, lands, and courts that were once thought to be eternal.

Crochet as an imitation lace also suffered a loss of popularity during this same period. Wearing crochet fell out of fashion in much the same way as wearing lace. Too many memories of class distinction were too fresh in the minds of people who no longer had to preserve a station in life and who were forging their own independence through hard-won victories.

In retrospect, the work accomplished by Mlle. Riego and other pioneers in crochet design became extremely important. They had already set the pace for design and expression of that design. Later, their printed instructions and design techniques helped to ensure the survival of crochet that generations of designers would pick up and follow many years later in England, throughout the European Continent, and in America.

Anne Orr, Mary Card, Sophie T. LaCroix, Frances A. Harris, Mary Fitch, Marie Antoinette, Augusta Pfeuffer, Winiford Worth, Adeline Cordet, Ema Farnes, Dorothy Bradford, Louise Nache, and Virginia Snow — all were important pioneer figures in American crochet design and publication. They were all skilled artists and educated women in the profession of textile design. Many were self-employed. Others worked for publishing companies or pattern-design firms. Crocheters were familiar with the designers of their era, and developed a true loyalty to their favorites.

Mary Card owned her own company and contributed to other publications. She was born in Australia and quickly became one of the most popular American designers. Mary Fitch was another popular designer who encouraged the continuation of ethnic techniques in crochet. She was particularly fond of the Irish Crochet.

Sophie T. LaCroix was a crochet lace designer who published many of her works in the publications of the "St. Louis Fancy Work." Augusta Pfeuffer also published her works in St. Louis. Emma Farnes was yet another of these popular designers who gained wide acclaim for her spider crochet patterns.

Sometimes, thread and other materials companies would publish their own extravagantly illustrated pattern books. They would feature

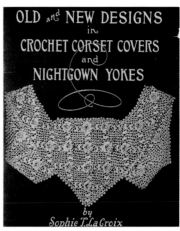

Crochet pattern books by American Crochet designers from the early 1900s. Private Collection, Annie Potter.

Crochet pattern books by Anne Orr, American designer of the early 1900s. Private Collection, Annie Potter.

Advertisements from an American needlecraft magazine during the early 1900s. Private Collection, Annie Potter.

their leading designer in those publications. Often the designers would become involved in the advertising plan for the publishing manufacturer. Frances Harris was one of the earliest designers who cooperated with the manufacturer to lend an "air of celebrity" to the company's advertising campaigns.

Anne Champe Orr was born at the end of the 19th Century and became one of America's most popular and prolific designers. Her career began at Coat's and Clark Thread Co., and her patterns were soon being featured as color center-folds on that manufacturer's pamphlets. While still a teenager, she was titled the principal editor and designer of Coat's and Clark needlework magazine. In 1919, she became Art Needlework editor of the "Good Housekeeping Magazine" and developed a loyalty among readers that lasted even after her death.

She also authored volumes of needlework patterns through her own publishing company, Anne Orr Studio of Nashville, Tennessee. Between 1910 and 1945, she published more than one hundred booklets that were to become rare collectors' items. In those publications, she assumed a high level of skill from her readers and often did not include the detailed instructions to which many needleworkers had grown accustomed. Later on, this presented a communication problem because the context of the terms that she used was not easily applicable to later generations.

Charted patterns were her specialty, and she graphed many designs for flowers, children, and animals. A unique process was used to ensure the practicability and accuracy of her design. A group of needlework experts, under her supervision, tested each design before publication.

She often borrowed ideas from Irish Crochet and Eastern European embroideries. Her publications were distributed in a number of foreign countries and became very popular. She designed collars, cuffs, centerpieces, doilies, and many other items that have proven to be timeless and sophisticated in concept and application. For example, some of her lingerie yokes are perfectly suitable for summer dresses.

Anne Orr helped chart the course for career women and she provided employment for many others. She worked continuously through her church and community for the benefit of still others. The Nashville Banner wrote, "She captured beauty from everything around her, and wove it into the tapestry of her life."

The late 20s and 30s meant hard times in America. The October Stock Market Crash on Black Tuesday resulted in a long depression putting 13 million people out of work. Even then, Americans had the spirit for fun and diversion. Crazy marathons were the rage. People danced. Sat in trees. Rode bikes until they fell exhausted.

During the early 20th Century, "The Modern Priscilla" was also a popular magazine that featured crochet instructions and tried to find new applications and projects. The magazine encouraged spontaneous creativity, and even suggested using materials that were uncommon during the time when filet crochet was so popular. The magazine, which cost two dollars a year or twenty cents an issue, also sponsored contests with cash prizes for winning crochet entrants.

There was a National crochet contest that was started in 1937 and continued through the 1940's which was sponsored by American crochet cotton manufacturers. Some of the designs hinted at the political issues of the day. In 1939, it was possible to see such entries as a crocheted airplane, American flags, and even President Roosevelt. The Crochet Speed Contest awarded the title of Lady Nimble Fingers to the crocheter who could produce the longest edging in an hour.

The events were popular enough to be covered by radio. That was quite an honor because the 30s and 40s represented the golden age of radio, and millions of Americans practiced a ritual of sitting around the "radio music box."

By the 1940s crochet was quite popular again; almost every home had a doily here and there. Heavier yarns had also become popular to

American pattern books representing the 1930s and the 1940s. Private Collection, Annie Potter.

create a new look for bedspreads and chairback covers.

In the 1950s, crochet garments similar to those being knitted were popular. Afghans, hats, shawls, and baby clothes were being made from cotton, wool, and even new synthetic threads. Designers and publishers were busy filling requests for patterns that could result in the creation

Typical American Crochet.

of an entire garment, not just result in trimming or insertion. Those were the days when there seemed to be plenty of time to crochet. World War II was over, and America was ready to relax, rely on tra-

Crochet speaking its international language. Turkish lady in the Istanbul airport shares crochet ideas with Annie Potter.

ditional values and customs, while enjoying the promise of bright economic future. Crochet in the 1960s embraced a new look — with new and unusual color combinations as well as different styles and applications. The crochet work captured the spirit of the times. The 60s — the so-called hippie era — was a time of miniskirts, jeans, ponchos, long hair, Vietnam, beads, and poems of peace. It was a time when people were intense about discovering new ways to do old things; a time when freedom in dress was considered to be a statement of independent thinking.

There was a heightened interest in producing things by hand during the decade of the 60s. This was happening at the same time that new, larger crochet hooks were also making the art seem new and fascinating. A grass roots fashion trend caught fire, and young people were busy crocheting their own version of a new style. They were soon followed by the older, more conservative people creating toned down versions of the new styles. It all happened so quickly that professional manufacturers and designers had to catch up to the fad that they did not initiate. Then, the manufacturers were trying to copy the popular handmade crochet look.

Since crochet was easy to learn, it didn't take weeks to complete a garment. The modern fashionable yarns that were perfect for the new look of the 60s were readily available. This crochet developed a free form aspect, reflected the times, and experimented with new ideas in the art of three dimensional pieces.

Men took an interest in the art, and its scope grew beyond the context of a vehicle for ladies to create "practical" articles for the home and family. However, this shouldn't seem too unusual to the modern mind that tries to box crochet into the parlor table with the "genteel" ladies. If the shepherds were the first to crochet, then men have played an integral part in its development since the beginning. Men crocheted in Ireland during the famine, and they have often won prizes in national contests. They are usually not bound by technique, tradition and pattern. Men have a natural tendency to explore potential and to approach the art with fresh eyes and a genuine sense of creativity.

Today — throughout America and throughout the world — women crochet for pleasure, relaxation, added income, for needlework cooperatives, and sometimes just to keep the crochet art alive. From China to Africa to the West

William Elmore, a modern American crochet designer, inventor and author, has a special flair for experimenting with colors and textures.

Yugoslavian folkwear costumes trimmed in crochet for the Zagreb Festival.

Indies, Jamaica, South America, Europe, and Asia, the crocheters are bound by a collective tradition and spurred by colonialism or missionary work or perhaps by the mysterious compulsion of man to create.

Crocheters are everywhere; in airports, market places, fairs, office buildings, universities, bus depots, remote street corners, isolated island villages, cloistered convents. Crochet speaks a language of its own; there's an immediate kinship among the women who love the art and take pride in what they accomplish. In many areas it is a social event, a time when women still get together to create, to compare, and to compete. Crochet is a hobby that can be developed from childhood to very old age... as long as the fingers can move.

"Modern" crochet appears in various forms and design all around the world. Many of the designs have been handed down generation to generation. Often, the pattern reflects the cultural heritage of a country and is unique there. Often, the local flavor is married to a traditional pattern design. Pattern designs are repeated in every art form, architecture, nature, grill work, art, or in any other way that allows the expression of fashion and trend.

Today's crocheters around the world are carrying into the 21st Century the direct relationship between design or patterns and a basic human need to "belong" to a larger group. Military uniforms, teams engaged in sports activities, men and women of certain religious orders, staff personnel of some business organizations, or the distinctive costumes from a specific region of a country all arrange dress patterns for a specific reason. There is a need to belong, or to identify with others having the same purpose, values, or culture.

Nowhere is this need more evident than in the folk costumes of people living all over the world. Some represent centuries of unbending traditions. Other costumes seem to explode with the dynamics of movement and improvisation. But common to all are the embellishments of design, color, and pattern that range from the raw and primitive to the more refined techniques achieved through centuries of tradition.

In the collective life of the village in Yugoslavia, for example, it was the woman who made the garments for her entire household. She grew, produced, and processed raw textile materials. Next, she produced them in brilliant colors, spun them, and used her looms to produce wool, linen, and even silk fabrics. Sewing and trimming the final garments often included pounding in pleats with rocks until the fabric fiber was broken enough to hold a permanent pleat. In some remote villages of that country, these ageless techniques are still being used today.

In Yugoslavia, for example, the cultural influence mixture is typical in various regional costumes heavily ornamented with crochet work along with lace, cut work, embroidery, and other woven designs. Zagreb, Dubrovnik, Zadar, Split, Pag, and others along the coastal routes of Yugoslavia take special pride in their rich cross-cultural heritage. Some of the finest laces and crochet work are still being produced by skilled craftsmen and women who carry on the traditions of a several millennia — work that rivals the fine, more publicized embroideries and laces of Western Europe,

such as Paris, Brussels, Vienna, Venice, and other pivotal centers of the art in the 20th Century. In fact, by creating unique and distinguished design, whole villages in Yugoslavia have supported themselves for centuries by turning out treasured crochet and lace pieces for eager markets.

The choice of materials, colors, blends of design, and patterns identify specific villages and are recognized immediately as belonging to that particular community. Within a village costume design, shades of meaning are built into the costumes. Rank, social status within the group, availability for marriage, and the trade or occupation of a person can be announced through pattern and symbol woven into the costume fabric or as part of its embellishment.

Crochet worker in the village of Pag, Yugoslavia.

Regional costumes and their trimmings also reveal much about the economy of the region, its climate, and its standard of living. Materials and techniques used to produce their clothing, and how they are worn, speak louder than any words. They also express feelings — happiness, sadness, joy, anticipation, and resolve. Truly, their costumes speak for them, and they are worn with pride.

At communal celebrations or even national festivals, folk costumes are brought out of old family trunks or closets and prepared for public display. In Zagreb, for example, an International Folklore Festival is held each year and provides an opportunity to share the mixtures of culture and performances from throughout the region. Knowing no national boundaries, people come from around the world to sing, dance, and share the ancient rituals and spirit of kinship with one another.

At each festival, there is singing of heroes, deeds of bravery, romantic notions, and the proverbs of accumulated wisdom. Spectators and participants alike are able to see and appreciate an astonishing display of costumes — filled with cut work, embroideries, crochet, and all types of ornamentation.

Imaginative patterns, motifs, designs, color, stitchery, different techniques, and innovations are worn. Each representative group provides insight into the deeply-felt traditions it holds. Each demonstrates its folk dances. Each has its own songs. Each has a unique flavor and style. Festivals are opportunities for sharing ideas, trading knowledge about people from distant places, and simply getting together to have fun.

Of particular interest to the history of both lace and crochet is the Adriatic island of Pag. A tiny dot on the map, this rocky and barren land off the coast of Yugoslavia and directly exposed to the cold winds sweeping down from Mt. Velebit, has been a center for the lace art for over four hundred years. Indeed, the whole economy of Pag has consistently depended upon the making of fine lace and also crochet for longer than perhaps any other community in the Western World. It is unique. Special. Very old.

The beauty and quality of workmanship in the needlework arts of Pag have become well-known far beyond the national boundaries of Yugoslavia. The rosette pattern has become a recognizable trademark of Pag lace and crochet, particularly in the past one hundred and fifty years.

The St. Mary's Church at the center of this small island community is described as having a front "Window of Lace" — to allow light and air to penetrate its interior. A tribute to the sculptor's art, the front wall has a large rosette cut into it. In a multi-layered style, the curved edges and design of this motif have been copied in the laces and crochet of the island ever since. Built in the year

1488, this church has recently celebrated its 500th Year Anniversary and has maintained a complete collection of what its people do best, crochet and lace. Rosettes can be found everywhere in the design of Pag laces and crochet as well as in its architecture, sculpture, metalwork, jewelry, and even on framework for arches and doorways. The motif even serves as a logo for the famous Pag cheese. Circular windows to let in the light, yet help maintain cool interiors, are as common as are the circular designs that are seen in their needlecraft being made on the streets.

Truly a "Crochet Village," Pag depends on its lace-making and crochet for its daily economic needs as well as its annual income. But, whereas its needlework was once aggressively exported along the trade routes of the Adriatic and into the far reaches of the Mediterranean and beyond, today's distributions have dwindled to the collectors and tourists who frequent the island in season. A traveler walking any lane or avenue in the village will see the men and women of Pag sitting in their doorways making lace and crochet pieces that they proudly display and sell.

One such woman of Pag had just celebrated her ninety-third birthday and was expertly turning out a new and magnificent piece of very fine lace. Her story is simple. Uncomplicated. She was born in the house behind her. Her family had lived there for nine hundred years. She had learned to make laces with bobbins and needles when she was four years old ... and has been doing it almost every day, all her life.

Her lament was that "the young people do not know how to do it...the art will die with me...but I know how important it has been...the lace...it has been good for me."

Among the finest laces and crochet work being produced anywhere in the world, the needlecrafts of Pag deserve a prominent place in the history and development of the needle arts.

Another outstanding example of the thriving antiquity of the needle arts in modern times would be Greece. The customs there provide

glimpses into not only common values held in modern times, but perhaps the best "living" perspective on a civilization that has endured for

Caves of Cappadocia, Turkey, still used for homes as they have been for centuries.

many thousands of years. Here, the living art of a people from pre-history to classical times — from old Byzantium and Turkish occupations.

For example, near Athens, on the tip of windy Cape Sounion, people gather at sunset as they have done for centuries... There, under the shadow of the blazing white doric columns of the ancient Temple of Poseidon, the mighty ancient God of Sea, fishermen continue to ready their nets for the evening catch, much in the same way as they have done for generations. Walking along the dock, legend of the creation of the fishing net echoes from boat to boat...legends of the sea...legends of the ancient sailors and their gods.

In Greece, the handicraft arts have reached many peaks of development over the centuries. The finest linens adorned ancient teachers, philosophers, and merchants.

Turkish woman in her Cappadocia Cave home shares her crochet work with Annie.

Often utilizing geometric and linear designs, Greek costumes are a kaleidoscope of color, embroidered

The Nuns of the Santa Florentina Convent in Spain crocheting in their patio, just as they have done for Centuries.

crosses, spirals, trees, leaves, suns, serpents, mythological monsters, gods, and birds. The island of Crete is a magical way to step back in time, to experience the art of crochet as it has existed for generations...men and women alike, anxious to share their heritage and their hospitality. Together, they produce and market their pieces in front of their homes or in the market place.

Originally inspired by ancient superstitions and faith in magical powers, Greek patterns and motifs have a sense of strength to them that is wrought by raised stitching, folds, pleats, and other devices of technique.

In many traditional costumes of Greece, a Moorish influence is obvious. Straight lines. Sharp points. Crisp edges. Masculine. In others, the softer and more refined look is apparent. Loosely draped folds. Sweeping lines of dresses caught at the shoulder. Beautifully woven sashes. Feminine.

Greek costumes for both men and women have shape and form that is ancient in origin. The classic wide-sleeved tunic has prevailed in Greece since at least 800 B.C. Gold or silver embroideries added as decor date back to the days of Homer.

Greek crochet and embroideries allow women to express their individual and creative spirit within a context of revered traditions and ancient culture. Handicrafts have been an integral part of the Greek dowry system, and the ability to perform a wide range of needle arts is a mark of both social and individual acceptance.

Still another culture, and another example of the living antiquity of the crochet arts in modern times is evident in the caves of Cappadocia, a village not far from the modern city of Ankara in Turkey. Cappadocia — a place of refuge for the persecuted Christians nine hundred years ago — is today, a dreamlike landscape, a place of mountainous beauty with ancient cave-like homes, hewn in the sides of the rocky formations, and still occupied as they have been for centuries. There are bizarre column-like formations with connecting narrow pathways between these ancient subterranean "cities" which thrive in the 20th Century. They have been carved deep into the ground and into the faces of towering spires and volcanic cones.

Here, time stands still. There have been few changes. The culture represents a melding of

Gazi, a modern university in the ancient city of Ankara, Turkey, continues to promote the art, appreciation and development of crochet and other needlecrafts reflecting mid-Eastern cultures.

today with very much the same lifestyles known many centuries ago. Palpable. Intriguing. Two or three generations of women sit on the side of the street to sell their crochet pieces to tourists...as they have for generations. For them, crochet represents a blueprint of their culture, a source of livelihood, and the artistic creation of their hand. Here, groups of women sit on their blankets beside a well-traveled road...tethered to the 20th Century, perhaps, by battery-powered radio or a television set prominently and proudly placed in a home that has been occupied by the same family for many generations.

Gazi University in Ankara supports the development of the crochet arts as a business within the University. The professors and students encourage and revere the continuation of ancient traditions in needlework, such as the activity at Cappadocia. They also plan the development of new design and technique which can be marketed on a global basis. Preservation. Pride. Economics. Creativity. All important elements in the developing mystery of timelessness that pervades the art of crochet in the 20th and 21st Centuries.

Crochet is timeless. The convents of Western Europe are where the art mysteriously evolved from the exotic laces and embroideries. A living example of the timelessness of the love of crochet in convents can still be found at the Santa Florentina Convent in Southern Spain.

As they have since the days of the Crusades, the nuns still sit in the shade of their convent patio behind the massive iron and wooden doors. Today, the Sisters crochet relatively undisturbed by the outside world and its frequent chaos.

They are carrying on the tradition of love in the creation of beauty for the Church, much as the nuns have done for centuries. Their work is unique and inspired. It deserves special attention as it represents a rich heritage that we all share in the history and art of crochet.

Crochet as it exists around the world today is unique, yet similar; exquisite, yet simple; traditional, yet innovative.

Today, the mysterious and magical potential of the art of crochet is still being discovered by many modern designers around the world. These very contemporary pieces are free-flowing and explode with experimentation in technique, yarn, form, application, and arrangement. Modern designers consider their crochet garments to be "wearable art," not merely crocheted clothing.

Many of these ultra-modern, 21st Century pieces are combined with leather and other popular fabrics to create new and exotic looks. These modern pieces exhibit a design sensitivity to the properties of crochet.

Today's crochet designers know how to study and take full advantage of the unique characteristics of crochet techniques. They are aware of the application of new and unusual materials, textiles, and fabrics to accomplish the concept of their design. Fabric painting and sculpture in crochet are more common now than ever before.

The craft is experimenting with design from the ancient patterns and studying techniques of the past. Designers mastered the basic principles of crochet that are necessary to ensure freedom and experimentation of form. They understand the continuity in the fascination of mankind for twisting, turning, looping, and creating.

Whatever beauty and freedom that one sees with the eye, or senses with the heart of an artist, can be transformed into crochet. Its history stretches back across time to the very earliest moments of existence. It is ageless. The need to create will keep it alive for uncounted generations to come. The mysterious fascination with the art continues.

New stories will evolve. Not content with what appears to be, researchers will continue to probe the mists of the past and gather strands of evidence that will shed new light on this very old textile form.

The meaning of history can only be found through individual interpretation of facts brought together in new ways. Many questions remain unanswered. Many secrets are yet to be opened. New dimensions to the creativity of the past are yet to be discovered. Crochet is more, far more, than a modern art form. It is an enduring heritage that forms a bridge between yesterday and tomorrow.

Exciting. Challenging. Profoundly important to the history of mankind. Enduring. Beautiful. As fresh today as ever. Flexible. Useful. Crochet indeed has its own place in history and its own unique heritage. It's a very special art form that often expresses the depths of inner feelings and the very soul of its makers. It is done with the heart and mind, as well as the hands.

You have taken a journey with me back through time. You have looked into the ages of history and have caught the important moments across the centuries when people discovered their own special ways to express themselves through their handicrafts from the earliest primitive forms of their art to the emergence of crochet as a special blend of skill, materials, and techniques.

The story of crochet is universal. It is deeply personal. It is a living mystery that still poses many unanswered questions. The quest for searching out and discovering new facets in the history and art of crochet is a continuing passion for many of us. We will carry on to probe the most remote corners of the world following the suggestions from our continuing research, as well as the dictates of our hearts as our amazing odyssey continues.

As the author of A Living Mystery: The International Art and History of Crochet , I would like to invite you now to come along with me on a pictorial journey through time and place - as my special guest.

Here in the warmth of the Santa Florentina Convent in Southern Spain, Annie discovered these nuns crocheting with the same traditions of love, beauty, and design that have characterized their work since the days of the 13th Century Great Crusades.

(Photos left) Walking the same ancient pathways that have been used by the hill peoples of mysterious Cappadocia, near Ankara, Turkey, for over 2,000 years, Annie shares her love of crochet with these men and women who depend upon their crochet skills for their livelihood. Still living in these caves these dedicated artisans work their crochet pieces in ancient designs and sell them to world travelers along narrow mountainous roadways. Here ancient cultures, and moslem traditions come together and remain basically unchanged over the centuries.

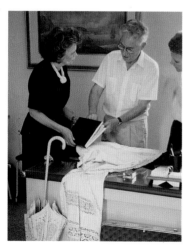

(Photos this page) Here on the Island of Crete, Annie uncovers the needlecraft secrets of Ancient Greece geometric styles and intricate designs, unique to the world. As they have done for generations, these warm and hospitable people fashion their crochet pieces in their doorways and in open air marketplaces. Traveling the world in the search for clues to uncover the true birth of crochet, Annie discovered incredible riches of ancient needlecraft history in the museums of Greece. Here, she found this amazing and exceedingly rare sample, documented as ancient Egyptian "threadwork." It constitutes priceless evidence that "stitching in the air" may have been known and practiced since the 900s AD. It represents a technique that could possibly be the earliest known predecessor of crochet. Annie Potter and John Sauer determine that this delicate fragment is identical in design to the modern Chevron Crochet Pattern.

At the Annual Zagreb Folk Festival in Yugoslavia, spectators and participants alike are able to appreciate an astonishing display of crochet and other needlearts that have been worked into rare costumes lovingly passed down through generations. Knowing no national boundaries, people gather here from throughout the world to sing, dance and share their ancient rituals in a spirit of kinship.

An authentic "crochet village" on the remote island of Pag, Yugoslavia. At the center of the village stands St. Mary's Church, famous for its "Window of Lace" which has provided a design pattern that can be found everywhere in the laces and crochet of Pag. Annie visits with ladies who sit outside the front doors of their homes along the narrow streets, selling their works as they have for many generations.

Left: Clones, an active commercial hub of Irish Crochet in the mid-1800s, is regaining its former stature, thanks primarily to people like Mrs D'Arcy, Ms. McDonald (pictured with Annie Potter at the Headquarters of the Crochet Guild and School in Clones) and Irish crochet historian and collector Nellie O'Clerich (pictured with Annie Potter) - these and others are leading the strong revival of Irish crochet into the 20th Century.

Right: Eithne D'Arcy, one of the most dedicated Irish crochet historians, author, collector, crochet designer and expert, shares her "treasures of lore" spanning three generations with Annie Potter.

James Walters and Sylvia Cosh are well-known modern English crochet designers who bring a freshness of spirit and totally new dimensions to the art. Here, in one of their many workshop/ seminars at Palace Castle, North Wales, they display their creative use of unique combinations of colors, textures and form, breathing new life into the modern magic of crochet.

Pauline Turner, English lecturer, designer and teacher of modern crochet, blends the mastery of traditional techniques with exciting new concepts for herself and her students.

An explosion of modern wardrobe fashion in crochet — new dimensions of the art that are at once beautiful, wearable, fashionable and elegant. New textures, colors and design combinations set the pace for the practical applications of modern crochet in the 21st Century. Compliments of Annie's Attic, Inc., Big Sandy, Texas.

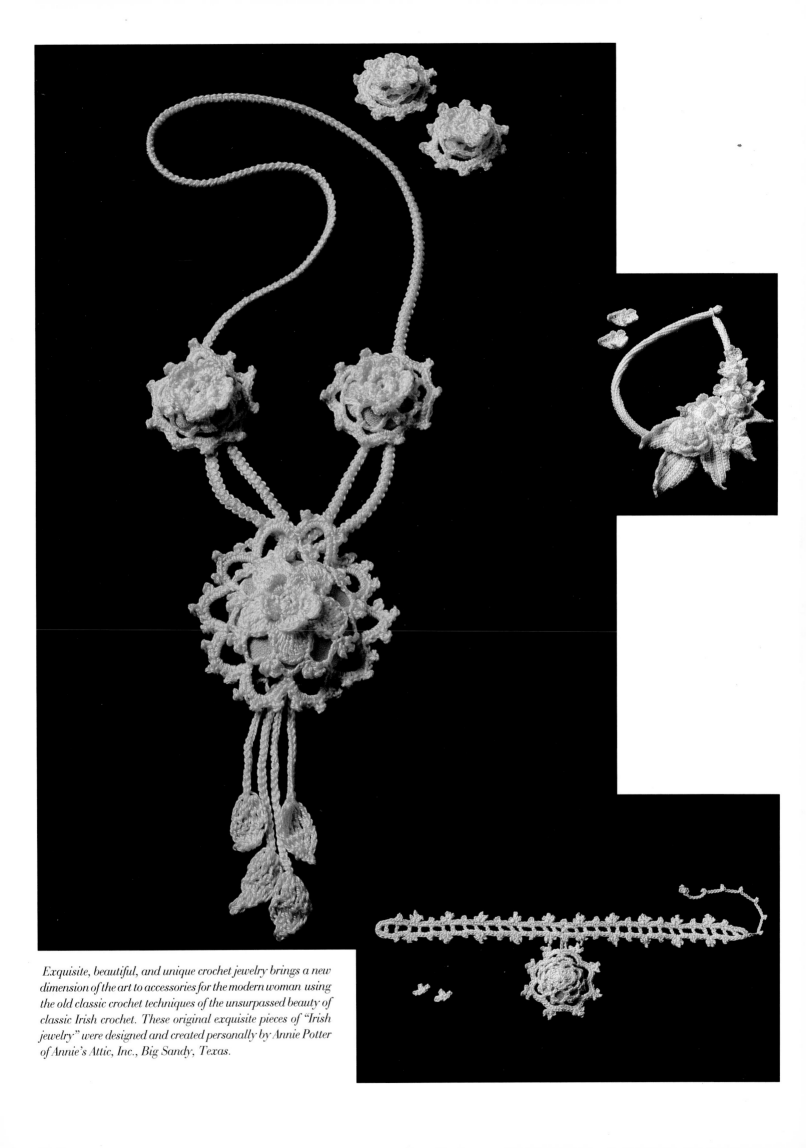

Exquisite, beautiful, and unique crochet jewelry brings a new dimension of the art to accessories for the modern woman using the old classic crochet techniques of the unsurpassed beauty of classic Irish crochet. These original exquisite pieces of "Irish jewelry" were designed and created personally by Annie Potter of Annie's Attic, Inc., Big Sandy, Texas.

A special request to my readers:

Many more facts and tales about Crochet and its story of love, poverty, pain and adventure remain in secret mystery. Together, let us continue to discover and share with each other the appreciation and development of this Art. My research team and I will continue searching, researching, and investigating worldwide in our endeavors to unravel more of the fascinating history and mystery of this exquisite craft.

If you have, or know about any special pieces or clues that would help complete our story — whether it be rare books, a letter, a manuscript, or a special antique piece of crochet — please share it with everyone by writing to me at: Annie's Attic, Inc., Corporate Offices, 222 W. Las Colinas Blvd. Suite l650, Irving, Texas 75039.

BIBLIOGRAPHY

A Winter Gift for Ladies. Philadelphia: J. & J.L. Gihon, 1850.

ACC Craft Fair, 1989 Directory of Exhibitors. Baltimore: American Craft Enterprises, Inc., 1989.

Alden, Cynthia-Westover, Women's Ways of Earning Money. New York: A.S. Barnes & Company.

Appel, John J. , From Shanties to Lace Curtains. Michigan: Michigan State University, 1971.

Arnold , Eleanor, Miss Arnold's Book of Crocheting, Knitting, and Drawn Work. Glasgow: Glasgow Lace and Thread Company, 1890.

Bagnall, William R., The Textile Industries of the United States. New York: Augustus M. Kelley, Publishers, 1893.

Bailey, Carolyn, Sherwin, What to do for Uncle Sam. Chicago: A. Flanagan Company, 1918.

Beard, Mary R., America Through Women's Eyes. New York: Greenwood Press, Publishers, 1933.

Beebe, C.D., Lace: Ancient and Modern. New York: Sharps Publishing Company, 1880.

Beecher, Catharine E., Treatise on Domestic Economy. Boston: Marsh, Capen, Lyon, and Webb, 1841.

Beecher, Catharine, E., and Harriet Beecher Stowe, The American Woman's Home. Hartford: Stowe-Day Foundation, 1869.

Benaki Museum, Athens, Greek Costumes and Embroideries. Washington: H.K. Press, 1959-1960.

Benson, Mary S., Ph.D., Women in Eighteenth Century America. NewYork: Columbia University Press, 1935.

Bevier, Isabel, Ph.M., and Susannah Usher, S.B., The Home Economics Movement: Part 1 Boston: Whitcomb & Barrows, 1906.

Bevier, Isabel, Ph.M., and Susannah Usher, S.B., The Home Economics Movement: Part 2. Boston: Whitcomb & Barrows, 1906.

Bisenic, Ljiljana, Vestina Kukicanja. Beograd: Niro Slobado, 1988.

Blaskovic, Vladimir, Zagreb. Zagreb: Graficki Zavod Hrvatske, 1976.

Blum, Clara, M., Old World Lace: A Guide for the Lace Lover. New York: E.P. Dutton, 1920.

Bowles, Ella, S., Homespun Handicrafts. Philadelphia: J.B. Lippicott Company, 1931.

Boyle, Elizabeth, The Irish Flowerers. Belfast: Queen's University, 1971.

Branchardiere, Riego de la, Eleonore, Irish Lace Instructor. London: Simpkin, Marshall, & Co., 1886.

Branchardiere, Riego de la, Eleonore, The Needle. London: Simpkin, Marshall, & Co., 1853.

Brittan, Judy, Good Housekeeping Step-by-Step Encyclopedia of Needlecraft. New York: Good House keeping Publications, 1980.

Brittan, Judy, The Bantam Step-by-Step Book of Needle Craft. Toronto: Bantam, 1979.

Broughton, Wynne, Crochet by Design. Pitman Publishing, 1976.

Bullock, Alice-May, Lace and Lacemaking. London: B.T. Batsford, Ltd., 1981.

Burton, Miss H., The Ladies Book of Knitting and Crochet. Boston: J. Henry Symonds, 1874.

Butler, Rudolph, Crocheting Machines. Germany, 1953.

Calhoun, Arthur W., Ph.D., A Social History of the American Family: From Colonial Times to the Present. New York: Barnes & Noble, Inc., 1917.

Can, Turhan, Turkey: Gate to the Orient. Istanbul: Orient Ltd., Company.

Caplin, Jessie F., The Lace Book. New York: MacMillan Company, 1932.Cave, Oenone.

Center for the History of American Needlework, Crochet Designs of Anne Orr. New York: Dover Publications, 1978.

Channer, C.C., and M.E. Roberts., Lace Making in the Midlands. London: Methuen & Co., 1900.

Channer, C.C., Lace Making in the Midlands Past and Present. London: Methuen & Co., 1900.

Clark, Graham, W.A., Lace Industry in England and France. Washington: Government Printing Office, 1909.

Cole, Arthur H., Ph.D., The American Wool Manufacture Volume I. Cambridge: Harvard University Press, 1926.

Collingwood, Peter, The Techniques of Sprang, Plaiting on Stretched Threads. London: Faber and Faber, Ltd., 1974.

Cordello, Becky Stevens, Editor, Needlework Classics. New York: Butterick Publishing, 1976.

Cowan, Ruth-Schwartz, More Work for Mother. New York: Basic Books, Inc., Publishers, 1983.

Craly, Jane-Cunningham, Knitting and Crochet: A Guide to the Use of the Needle and the Hook. Lynn: J.F. Ingalls, Pub., 1886.

Cut-Work Embroidery and How to Do It. New York: Dover Publications, Inc., 1963 (1983 by Dover).

Dale, Julie Schafler, Art To Wear. New York: Abbeville Press, 1986.

Dawson, Pam (Editor), Monarch Illustrated Guide to Crochet. New York: Monarch Press, 1977.

Demir, Omer, Cappadocia: Cradle of History. Ankara, Turkey: Ajans-Turk Publishing & Printing Co., Inc., 1988.

Dubois, Jean, Anne Orr Patchwork. Durango: La Plaza Press, 1977.

Earle, Alice M., Customs and Fashions in Old New England. Massachusetts: Corner House Publishers, 1969.

Earnshaw, Pat, Needle-Made Laces: Materials, Designs, Techniques. London: Ward Lock Limited, 1988.

Earnshaw, Pat, Youghal and Other Irish Laces. Guildford: Gorse Publications, 1988.

Enrenber, Margaret, Women in Prehistory. British Museum Publications, Ltd., 1989.

Ellet, Elizabeth F., The Pioneer Women of the West. New York: Books for Libraries Press, 1852.

Feldman, Annette, Handmade Lace and Patterns. New York: Harper & Row, Publishers, 1975.

Feldmann, Del P., The Crocheter's Art. New York: Doubleday & Company, Inc., 1974.

Fisher, Joan, Guide to Needlecraft. London: Trewin Copplestone Publishing, Ltd., 1972.

Fowler, William W., Woman on the American Frontier. Hartford: S.S. Scranton & Co., 1876.

Frank Leslie's Portfolio of Fancy Needlework. New York: Stringer and Townsend, 1885.

Frost, Annie S., The Ladies Guide to Needle Work, Embroidery, Etc... New York: Adams & Bishop, Publishers, 1877.

Fuchs, Heide, and Maria Natter, Laclamke Ljubljana: Mladinska Knijiga, 1988.

Golta, Thomas, (Ed.), Istanbul Singapore: APA Publications, Ltd., 1988.

Graves, Sylvia, Needlework Tools and Accessories. London, 1966

Guild of Irish Lace Makers, Irish Lace Journal, Spring 1989.

Habler, O., Textile Art and Industry East Germany: Hugo Willisch, 1916.

Hale, Sarah J., Manners: or Happy Homes and Good Society. New York: Arno Press, 1867.

Hall, Florence H., Social Customs. Boston: Estes and Lauriat, 1887.

Handarbeiten, Mehr Freude mit, SVE o Rucnmim Radovima Zurich: Droemersche Verlagsanstalt Th. Knaur Nachg, 1979.

Holiday, Carl, Woman's Life in Colonial Days. Detroit: Gale Research Company, 1970.

Household Leaves: A Manual of Knitting and Crocheting. Mass: Household Publishing, 1887.

Howard, Constance, Textile Crafts. New York: Charles Scribner's Sons, 1978.

Hrbud, Josip, Folklor Naroda Jugoslavije. Zagreb: Grafickog Zavoda Hrvatske, 1963.

Huetson, T.L., Lace and Bobbins: A History and Collectors Guide. Vermont: David and Charles, Inc., 1973. New Edition, 1983.

Illustrated Manual of Knit and Crochet. New York: M. Hemingway and Sons, 1889.

Ireland of the Welcomes. January-February, 1989, Volume 38, No. 1.

Ivancevic, Radovan, Art Treasures of Croatia. Belgrade: Jugoslovenska, 1986.

Jackson, F. Nevill, A History of Hand Made Lace. Smithsonian Institute Library.

Jeffery, Julie, Roy, Frontier Women: The Trans Mississippi West. New York: Hill and Wang, 1979.

Jourdain, Margaret, Old Lace: A Handbook for Collectors. London: B.T. Batsford, Ltd., 1988.

Kent, Muriel, Exciting Crochet: A Course in Broomstich and Tunisian Crochet. Pomfret: David and Charles, 1977.

King, Elizabeth, Crochet Book. New York: Leisure League of America,1935.

Klickmann, Flora, The Ambition of Jenny Ingram: A True Story of Modern Life. London, 1907.

Kofou, Anna, Crete: All the Museums and Archeological Sites. Athens: Ekdotike Athenos S.A., 1989.

Konior, Mary, Heritage Crochet: An Analysis. London: Dryad Press, Ltd., 1987.

Kraatz, Anne, Lace: History and Fashion. New York: Rixxoli, 1989.

Lace Crafts Quarterly. Volume 2, #1, Spring, 1989.

Ladies Work-Table Book: Instruction in Plain and Fancy Needlework. Philadelphia: T.B. Peterson, 1850.

Ladies' Self Instructor in Millinery and Mantua Making. Philadelphia: Leary & Getz, 1853.

Lambert (Ref.: Miss Lambert), The Hand-Book of Needlework. New York: Wiley & Putnam, 1847.

Lane, Rose Wilder, Book of American Needlework. New York: Fireside Book Publishing, 1961, 1962, 1963.

Laury, Jean R., and Joyce Aiken, Creating Body Coverings. New York: Van Nostrand Reinhold Company, 1973.

Lowes (Ref: Mrs. Lowes), Chats On Old Lace and Needlework. London: T. Fisher Unwin, 1908.

MacDonald, Anne L., No Idle Hands: The Social History of American Knitting. New York: Ballantine Books, 1988.

Maines, Rachel, American Needlework in Transition 1888-1930. Center for the History of American Needle work, Dacus Library, Winthrop College, 1977.

Matthews, Anne L., Vogue Dictionary of Crochet Stitch. Pomfret: David and Charles, 1987.

May, Florence L., Hispanic Lace and Lace Making. New York: Printed by Order of the Trustees, Hispanic Society of American, 1939.

Mee, Cornelia, A Manual of Knitting, Netting and Crochet. London: David Grague, 1844.

Mendoza, Cristina y Eduardo, Ciudades en la Historia. Barcelona: Editorial Planeta, 1989.

Museus, Junata de, Catalog. Barcelona: Paulau de Pedralbes, 1933.

Needle and Hook. New York: Belding Brothers, 1895.

Needle at Home: A Complete Instruction to Branches of Plain and Fancy Needle Work. Springfield: Franklin Fromer, 1885.

O'Cleirigh, Nellie, Carrickmacross Lace. London: Dryad Press Ltd., 1985.

O'Connell, Michael, Shadows: An Album of the Irish People 1841-1914. Dublin: The O'Brien Press, 1985.

Onuk, Doc. Taciser, Igne Oyalari Needleworks. Ankara: Dogus Matbaacilik ve Tic. Ltd. St1, 1988.

Pond, Gabrielle, An Introduction to Lace. New York: Charles Scribner's Sons, 1973.

Primitive Scandinavian Textiles in Knotless Netting. Norway: Oslo University Press, 1961.

Pullman, Mrs; (Ref: Mrs. Warren), Treasure in Needle work. New York: Berkley Windhover Book, 1976.

Rathbone, Iris, Crochet: A Modern Guide to Ancient Craft. John Gifford, Ltd., 1968.

Rettlers, Lina, Penelope Knitting and Crochet Series: Books 1 & 2. Brooklyn: The Misses Stock, 1885.

Righetti, Maggie, Crocheting in Plain English. New York: St. Martin's Press, 1988.

Rogers, Gay A., An Illustrated History of Needlework Tools. London: John Murray Publishers, Ltd., 1983.

Ryan, Richard, A History of Hand Knitting. Loveland: Interweave Press, 1987.

Simeon, M., History of Lace. London: Stainer &Bell, 1979.

Smith, Doris, M., Encyclopedia of Crochet Patterns, Stitches and Designs. Georgia: FC&A, Inc., 1988.

Smithsonian Institution's National Museum of Design, Lace. Washington, D.C.: Smithsonian Institution., 1982.

Solunac, Tanja, and Ana Sretenovic, Zlatna Petlja. Beograd: Kosmos, 1988.

Sommer, Elyse, and Mile Sommer, A New Look Crochet. New York: Crown Publishers, Inc., 1975.

Spenceley, G.F.R., English Pillow Lace Industry. London: Hull University, 1979.

Stearns, Ann, The Batsford Book of Crochet. London: B.T. Batsford, Ltd., 1981.

Stevenson, Isabelle, Crochet and Knitting for Every Woman. Chicago: Peoples Book Club, 1947.

Taylor, Gertrude, American Crochet Book. New York: Charles Scribner's Sons, 1972.

The Last and Best Book on Knitting, Crocheting, Embroidery: Art Needlework. New York: Brainer & Armstrong Company, 1892.

Tilke, Max, Costumer Patterns and Designs. London: A Zwemmer, Ltd.,1956.

Titiana, Ioannov-Yannara , Greek Threadwork-Lace. Athens: Melissa Publishing House, 1989.

Turner, Pauline, Crochet: A History of the Craft Since 1850. Haverfordwest: Shire Publications, Ltd., 1984.

Vecellio, Cesare, Pattern Book for Renaissance Lace. New York: Dover Publications, Inc., 1988.

Walker, C.B.F., Cuneiform. British Museum Publications, Ltd., 1987.

Walters, James, and Sylvia Cosh, Crochet. London: Octopus Books, Ltd., 1980.

Wardle, Patricia, Victorian Lace. Carlton & Bedford, 1982.

Weldon and Company, Victorian Crochet. New York: Dover Publications, Inc., 1974.

Woman's Day Book of Granny Squares. New York: Simon and Schuster, 1975.

Yung, K.K., Complete Illustrated Catalogue - 1856-1979. London: National Portrait Gallery, 1981.

Zdunic, Drago, The Folk Costumes of Croatia. Spektar: Zagreb, 1975.

Zunic-Bas, Leposava, Folk Traditions in Yugoslavia Ten Tours. Jugoslavija: Izdavacki Zavod, 1973.